Lernthriller Englisch

IN TERR

Sarah Trenker

compact

Weitere Informationen zu Compact Lernthriller finden Sie am Ende des Buches und unter www.lernkrimi.de.

Baierbrunner Straße 27, 81379 München
Ausgabe 2012

Chefredaktion: Dr. Matthias Feldbaum
Redaktion: Helga Aichele, Ursula Bachhausen
Fachkorrektur: Nathalie Russell
Produktion: Johannes Buchmann
Titelabbildung: fotolia.com, ping han
Lernkrimi-Logo: Carsten Abelbeck
Gestaltung: EKH Werbeagentur Gbr, textum GmbH
Umschlaggestaltung: EKH Werbeagentur Gbr, Hartmut Baier

ISBN 978-3-8174-8857-5
381748857/1

www.compactverlag.de, www.lernkrimi.de

VORWORT

Liebe Leserin, lieber Leser,

mitreißend und unheimlich spannend – die Compact Lernthriller mit ihrer Kombination aus fesselnder Lektüre und didaktischem Übungsanteil eignen sich hervorragend, um breite Sprachkompetenzen in der Fremdsprache zu erwerben. Der Lerner wird dabei durch die atemberaubende Handlung, das angemessene Sprachniveau und den stetig ansteigenden Schwierigkeitsgrad der Übungen gefördert und motiviert. Ein ausführlicher Abschlusstest ermöglicht das Wiederholen und Festigen des Gelernten. In einem alphabetischen Glossar am Ende des Buches sind noch einmal übersichtlich alle Vokabeln zum Nachschlagen aufgelistet.

So lernen Sie mit Compact Lernlektüren:

- **Mit Begeisterung lernen:** Die packende Handlung motiviert Sie beim Lesen des englischen Originaltextes.
- **Wissen intensivieren und erweitern:** Durch die Kombination aus didaktisierter Lektüre und textbezogenen Übungen testen und trainieren Sie Ihre Sprachkenntnisse effektiv. Vokabelangaben auf jeder Seite unterstützen Sie beim Lesen.
- **Systematisch lernen:** Knüpfen Sie an Ihr individuelles Sprachniveau an und setzen Sie eigene Lernziele – linear im Schwierigkeitsgrad ansteigend oder mit punktuellen Schwerpunkten von Grundwortschatz bis Hörverstehen.
- **Unabhängig sein:** Lernen Sie ganz individuell – wo und wann Sie wollen.

Viel Spaß beim **spannend Englisch lernen**
wünscht Ihnen

Prof. Dr. Christiane Neveling
Didaktik der romanischen Sprachen, Universität Leipzig

INHALT

ZU DIESEM BUCH

Eine junge Frau erwacht im Krankenhaus ohne Gedächtnis. Als sie wegen Mordes verhaftet werden soll, flieht sie voller Panik an die englische Südküste – die Polizei dicht auf ihren Fersen. Ist sie wirklich eine Mörderin? Erste Erinnerungen kehren zurück und sie versucht verzweifelt, das Rätsel um ihre Identität zu lösen. Doch wem kann sie trauen?

1 DRUGS AND ROCK 'N' ROLL

When she woke up, there were blue and purple lights flashing in front of her eyes – and she seemed to be dancing. It was a strange sensation, especially since her eyes were closed and she could not move. It was like being fully awake in a dream. A voice inside her head was speaking to her, but she could not hear it properly.

After a while, she realized that she was on her own in a room, but she could hear other people nearby. There was a horribly strong smell of disinfectant. Tight sheets held her body, but there was no pain. Still sleepy, she wondered whether that was good or bad. Had she had an accident? Was she paralyzed? Or was she just in shock? She could not remember an accident. She searched slowly through the empty chambers of her brain for more information. Shocked, she realized that it was not just the accident that she could not remember: she could not remember anything at all. Who was she? Why was she here?

to flash	blitzen
disinfectant	Desinfektionsmittel
paralyzed	gelähmt
twitch	Zucken

She tried again to open her eyes, but it was as if they were glued together, like her lips. She tried to move her hand, but managed only a tiny twitch in her fingers. She was trapped inside her own body.

Fear began to spread through her body. She was literally petrified – in every sense of the word.

A door opened and she heard the steps of two people. They came over to where she was lying, and she felt someone pick up her wrist to feel her pulse. They both had the perfumed smell of women and the hand holding her wrist was soft. On the other side of the bed, she felt the sheet being pulled even tighter across her breast.

Esther tried but could not speak or communicate in any way that she was awake.

After a minute, the owner of the soft hands spoke. "Her pulse is normal. I think that she'll wake up soon."

"You're kidding," laughed the woman on the left-hand side of the bed. "Dr Michael said that she's drugged up to the eyeballs. She swallowed enough pills to wipe out a battalion. It's a surprise that she's here at all."

"Who would have thought it? That Esther Radcliffe is into drugs! And that someone who sings such beautiful love songs would be capable of murder..."

"Well, they always say that love and hate are very close together. Perhaps she was in love with Paul Tyne. He was certainly extremely good-looking."

"Such a waste," the other nurse sighed, as she continued to straighten the bed.

"Yes, in many ways. And who will the up-and-coming star sing for when she is doing time – her fans in prison?"

"Oh Beth, you are awful!"

literally	buchstäblich, wortwörtlich
petrified	versteinert, starr vor Angst
↯ drugged up to the eyeballs	total zugedröhnt
↯ to be into sth.	auf etw. stehen/abfahren
to be capable of	fähig sein
up-and-coming star	Nachwuchsstar
↯ to do time	im Gefängnis sitzen

Both nurses **giggled**. Then Beth spoke more seriously. "Go and tell the young policeman in the canteen that she will **be coming round** soon. He should be standing outside the door when she does."
"But he has only just gone down to the canteen."
"Well, he has got about an hour, so he can eat in peace. Or perhaps you'd like to keep him company…? Don't think I didn't see you both flirting earlier!"
Another giggle. "He is really good-looking, isn't he?"

to giggle	kichern
to come round	zu sich kommen
relieved	erleichtert
detached	losgelöst, unbeteiligt
to sink in	wirken, ins Bewusstsein dringen
limbs *pl*	Gliedmaßen

Beth sighed. "But be careful this time, Susie, won't you? Don't jump in with both feet again."
The door shut before anything else was said.
My name is Esther Radcliffe, and I am a singer and a murderer, thought the woman lying in the bed. Soon I will be able to move, and then they will put me in prison. At first, the thoughts did not really affect her. She was **relieved** that now she at least knew her name, but she felt very **detached** from the woman the nurses had been talking about. However, as the thoughts began to **sink in**, the fear came back. Panic pumped through her body.

Vorsicht mit **affect** und **effect:**
to affect sb.
jdn. betreffen, sich auf jdn. auswirken (häufig negativ)
to have an effect on sb.
jdn. beeinflussen, sich auf jdn. auswirken

Suddenly she could hear a voice echoing in the empty cave of her brain: "They have to be wrong. You need time, time to remember, to remember, to remember. You have to get away, get away, get away…"
Her **limbs** needed to follow her brain's instructions. Concentrating all her efforts on her fingers, Esther Radcliffe slowly managed

to lift her right hand off the bed. She did the same with her left hand and then began to open and close both hands before starting the same process with her feet. It seemed to take forever.

Exercise 1: Question tags. **Formulieren Sie Frageanhängsel zu folgenden Sätzen!**

1. The nurse is a bit of a dragon, ______________________?
2. She didn't really kill Paul Tyne, ______________________?
3. You've taken her pulse, ______________________?
4. She wouldn't do such a thing, ______________________?
5. I'm wrong to think that, ______________________?

"The policeman will be here soon," the voice screamed. "Then you will be trapped. Hurry up, hurry up. Get out, get out!"
Every noise outside the door made her try harder. The adrenalin seemed to reach her eyes because suddenly they were open, and she found herself staring at a yellow ceiling with a long neon lamp. She moved her head slightly to look to the left. She saw a washbasin, a small white cabinet, a chair and a big window. Next to the bed was a stand holding an infusion, which was attached to her left arm.
At a snail's pace, she moved her head to the right. She was on her own in the room. The door was still shut. It did not have a window, so she could not see if the policeman was already standing outside. Panic flooded her again. She had to get out. How long had it been since the nurses left? Five minutes, half an hour, an hour?
Gritting her teeth together, she focused on her right arm again. "Move, damn you," she shouted, though luckily it only came out

as a murmur. Her right arm obeyed her, and she was able to lift her whole arm off the bed. Again, she repeated the process with the left arm, her right leg, her left leg. "How much time is left?" shouted the voice. "Are you going to get away in time?" Esther could feel sweat running down her back. Her breathing was heavier. Suddenly, the adrenalin seemed to break through the paralysis. From one second to the next, she could move quite normally.
Pulling herself up in the bed, she looked at the infusion tube in her left arm. Her fingers were trembling. For some reason that she could not remember, she knew how to remove the tube. She found a plaster on top of the cabinet, which she put over the small wound.
There was movement outside the door and she froze for a second.
"People, people, hide, hide," shouted the voice.
Automatically, she stuck the infusion tube under the plaster, lay down and closed her eyes. The door opened, but no one walked in.
"She still looks dead to the world," Esther heard a man say.
"That would be a good title for her next song," a woman said dryly.
Esther recognized the woman's voice; it was the younger of the two nurses: Susie. She wondered if the man was the policeman.
As if to answer her question, the man added, "Her clothes should be with forensics by now. I'd better call the station again."
The door shut.
Esther opened her eyes again. Red and purple lights flashed before her eyes. She felt dizzy

at a snail's pace	im Schneckentempo
to flood	durchfluten, überfluten
to grit one's teeth	die Zähne zusammenbeißen
murmur	Murmeln
to freeze	*hier*: erstarren
ϟ dead to the world	total hinüber
forensics	Spurensicherung; Rechtsmedizin
dizzy	schwindelig

Exercise 2: Idioms. Ergänzen Sie diese Redewendungen mit „time"!

in | take | matter | against

1. Will she be able to get away ______ time?
2. She is in a race ______ time.
3. Hopefully, the policeman will ______ his time in the canteen.
4. It is only a ______ of time before the nurses return.

"The policeman is already outside the door. You were too slow," the voice mocked. "Your only chance is the window. Why don't you try to fly again?"
"Shut up and let me think," Esther replied in an angry whisper.
She sat up again. What floor was she on? Could she jump? Could she even get out of bed?
Again, she heard people outside the door. She listened for a second, but it was just Susie and the policeman chatting. Perhaps the flirtatious nurse would be her ticket to freedom. She had to act quickly.
"Quickly? You are joking, aren't you!" laughed the voice.
Esther ignored it, ignored the flashing colours and the dizziness. She was in control. It was HER body.
She looked around the room again. Some clothes were lying over the back of a chair. She did not recognize them, but she guessed they were hers: a black evening dress and high-heeled shoes.

"How practical," the voice mocked.
Frowning, Esther swung her legs over the side of the bed and slowly stood up. She was dizzy, but she was able to get to the chair without falling over. She pulled on the dress as quickly as she could, ignored the shoes and then walked back and forth for a minute until she was sure of her balance. Finally, she walked over to the window. Her heart sank when she looked out. She was at least four flights up. Below she saw a large, luckily deserted space full of big plastic bins of different colours.

flirtatious	kokett
to frown	die Stirn runzeln
Her heart sank.	Ihr rutschte das Herz in die Hose.
flight	*hier*: Stockwerk
ledge	Sims
to peer	spähen
to hitch up	hochziehen

"Ha, ha, ha! I said you should fly…"
Esther shook her head angrily. She leant out of the window and saw that there was a ledge beneath it. It was wide enough for her to stand on. She peered along the wall, hoping to find a fire escape, but could see nothing, just other windows.
"Fly, fly away… Let's fly, fly away," sang the voice in time to the flashing colours in front of her eyes.
She had to block out the voice somehow. It was making her mad. Or was she already mad?
Susie was still talking to the young policeman, but how much longer would it be before the nurse had to get back to work? This was her only option. She had to give it a try.
Hitching up her dress, Esther climbed out of the window and onto the ledge, holding on to the window frame all the time. Looking up, she noticed that there was another ledge above her head that she could hold on to. As there was only one window to pass before she came to the corner of the building on the right, she decided to go that way. Perhaps she would find a fire escape around the corner.

Slowly she transferred one hand and then the other to the ledge above her head. To stop the dizziness, she stared at the wall, telling herself not to look down because then she would surely fall.
"Fly, fly away," **hummed** the voice inside her head.
"Stop it," she begged. "Leave me alone."

to hum	summen
courtyard	(Innen)Hof
start	*hier:* Aufschrecken

Painfully slowly, she moved along the ledge. A loose stone fell off the ledge and dropped to the **courtyard** below. For a moment, Esther was paralyzed with fear again. She closed her eyes, but the dancing lights immediately came back, so she quickly opened them again.
"Come on, Esther – whoever you are. You can do it. There are only a couple of more steps to the window."
"Yeah, fly, fly away," answered the voice.

Exercise 3: Vocabulary quiz. Ergänzen Sie die Aussagen und enträtseln Sie das Lösungswort!

1. At first, Esther cannot □ _ _ _ her limbs.
2. The voice inside her head tells her to _ □ _ _ _ up.
3. She cannot _ _ _ _ _ _ _ □ what happened.
4. The only escape is through the _ _ _ □ _ _.
5. Paul Tyne is _ □ _ _.
6. The policeman is talking to a _ _ □ _ _.

Lösung: _ _ _ _ _ _

Suddenly Esther stopped. What would she do if somebody was standing at the window? She looked back. No, passing the window was still her only option. She looked up and saw that the ledge continued above the window. She had got this far, so it had to be possible to go on! Gritting her teeth, Esther moved another two steps along the ledge in front of the window. Risking a look inside, she saw that there were two beds in the room.

Exercise 4: Choose the correct alternative. Lesen Sie weiter und unterstreichen Sie die richtige Variante!

In the bed next to the window was a woman with a **1.** broken / broke leg. She was **2.** deep / fast asleep. Good. Then Esther's eyes moved over to the other bed. With a **start** that almost caused her to **3.** lose / loose her grip, she saw that the old woman sitting in that bed was staring right at her.

Time stood still for a couple of seconds. Then the old woman waved and smiled **4.** happily / happy. Esther let out her breath again. Yes, the world had definitely gone mad. Then she continued moving along the ledge, not taking her eyes **5.** of / off the woman, who continued to smile and wave **6.** at / to her.

"This is madness, absolute madness," Esther murmured to herself.
And what was she going to do if there was no way down? As she reached the corner of the building, she said another little prayer. "Please, please, let there be a fire escape."
She peered around the corner and almost shouted in frustration. There *was* a fire escape, but it was directly above a main entrance, and there were many people around. There was no way she could get to it unseen.
"And now?" the voice **taunted**.
I have no choice, thought Esther desperately. She could not go forward, so she would have to go back. Slowly, Esther turned back. The muscles in her arms were aching, and she knew that there was no way she would be able to continue for much longer. Perspiration and tears of frustration flowed down her cheeks. As she reached the first window, she saw that the old lady was still looking out, and that she waved again when she saw Esther.

to taunt	verhöhnen, sticheln
ϟ nutty as a fruitcake	total verrückt
to have a go	etw. ausprobieren
to lock sb. up	jdn. einsperren, jdn. wegsperren
clothes locker	Spind

Esther could not smile back. The woman got out of bed, walked over to look at Esther more closely and then opened the window. Esther did not know whether to laugh or continue crying. She could not believe her luck.
"Why are you crying? Won't anybody play with you?" the woman asked excitedly, jumping up and down like a child and clapping her hands.
"**Nutty as a fruit cake**," said the voice in her head.
"Yes – thank God!" Esther thought to herself as she quickly climbed into the room. She put her finger over her mouth.

"Shh, we'll wake her up," she said, pointing at the woman sleeping in the other bed.
"Oh no, we won't," the old lady giggled toothlessly. "They have just given her pills to make her sleep."
The old lady continued hopping from one foot to the other. "It must be frightening walking along that ledge. Can I **have a go**?"
"It is very frightening," replied Esther. "I don't think you should try it. I am hiding from someone sitting in front of my door. He and his friends want to **lock me up**."
"Yes, they did that to me, too," replied the old woman, suddenly serious. "They took away my house and put me in a small room somewhere out in the countryside. I can't get away either."
Not really listening, Esther looked wildly around her. She opened a **clothes locker** next to the bathroom door and saw some jeans and a jumper. She held up the jeans against her body. They might fit her.
"You can't hide in the locker," observed the old woman. "It is too small."
"I need a disguise," Esther said and took the other clothes out of the locker. "If I leave the room in this dress, they will recognize me."

Exercise 5: Synonyms. Welche Wörter gehören zusammen? Ordnen Sie zu!

1. ☐ tremble	a) taunt
2. ☐ petrified	b) mad
3. ☐ mock	c) terrified
4. ☐ ache	d) shake
5. ☐ nutty	e) hurt

"It's like the war," the old lady said, giggling happily again. "Hide in the bathroom and change quickly. The guards will be coming in soon." As she said that, they both heard the sound of a trolley being pushed towards the door. Esther ran into the bathroom and closed the door. She sank down in the corner and closed her eyes again. The dizziness returned immediately. Outside, she heard the door to the room open and someone walk in.

"Hello, Mrs Anderson," said a friendly male voice. "I hope you're hungry today. It's your favourite – trifle."[i]

Trifle ist eine typische englische Süßspeise, bestehend aus mehreren Schichten aus Vanillesoße, Obst oder Marmelade, Biskuitboden und Schlagsahne.

"Nobody wants me anymore," the old lady grumbled. "My son sent me away and now you are sending me back to Mary's Lodge, too."

"Come on, Mrs Anderson." The voice was soothing but firm at the same time. "Get back into bed. You don't want me to fetch the nurse, do you?"

Esther only started breathing again when she heard the door shut. Had they discovered that she was no longer in her room? How was she going to get out into the corridor without being seen?

She looked at herself in the mirror. The face she saw was somehow familiar. It was like seeing someone in a restaurant and realizing that you know them but can't remember where and when you met.

Her hair was jet black and her eyes a startling green. It would be easy for people to identify her.

to grumble	brummen, murren
soothing	beruhigend
firm	fest, bestimmt
jet black	kohlrabenschwarz
startling	*hier*: außergewöhnlich
strand	*hier*: Strähne
beret	Baskenmütze
crumpled	zerknüllt

She pulled on the jeans, jumper and shoes that she had found in the locker. Luckily, the shoes were more or less the right size.
The door to the bathroom opened, and Esther started. But it was only the old woman, Mrs Anderson.
"He's gone," she giggled. "Why are they looking for you anyway?"
Esther trembled. "I don't really know. I can't remember."

Exercise 6: Translation. Übersetzen Sie die englischen Verben!

1. recognize ______________________
2. giggle ______________________
3. hide ______________________
4. soothe ______________________
5. frown ______________________

"I can't remember a lot of things either these days," Mrs Anderson sighed sadly, pushing a strand of hair out of her face. "But you are still very young. Perhaps something horrible happened to you. If you think about it for long enough, you will probably remember... Anyway, you'd better take these."
She smiled a little wildly again and handed Esther a red beret, a pair of dark glasses and a crumpled fifty-pound note.
Pulling on the beret and the glasses, Esther went over to the door. Trembling from head to toe, she opened the door just enough to look out into the corridor.
Her inner voice was suddenly positive. "You're in luck. Come on – go, go, go!"

Esther assessed the situation as quickly as she could. To fight the dizziness, she closed her eyes briefly and then opened them again. On the right, there was a group of doctors talking. They were standing between her and the policeman. He was now alone and sat in front of her room reading a newspaper.
Esther walked out into the corridor and headed as normally as she could in the other direction. It seemed to take forever before she could turn a corner.
"Excuse me, may I ask where you are going?"
Esther froze and turned round to find a nurse looking at her.

Exercise 7: Reported speech. Wandeln Sie die Sätze in indirekte Rede um!

1. "I can't remember a lot of things these days," she said.
   She said that she couldn't remember a lot of things these days.
2. "What are you going to do?" she asked her.
   She asked her ____________________
3. "They will take her home soon," he said.
   He said that ____________________
4. She said, "People in disguise always wear a hat."
   ____
5. She said, "You are very young."
   ____

"I was just trying to find the exit," she stuttered.

"Well, it's not here. It's on the opposite side of the corridor, where it says 'Exit'," the nurse replied sarcastically. Then she looked at Esther more closely. "Don't I know you?"

Esther recognized the voice. It was one of the nurses who had been in her room – Beth, she supposed.

"We spoke the other day," Esther answered quickly.

"Oh yes...," the nurse replied, looking a little confused.

to assess	abschätzen, einschätzen
to head (towards)	eine Richtung ansteuern
briskly	rasch, flott

Exercise 8: Verb forms. Lesen Sie weiter und setzen Sie die korrekte Verbform ein!

Esther **1.** turn ______________ and walked towards the exit as **briskly** as she **2.** can ______________. Any second now they would **3.** discover ______________ that she had disappeared and then escape would be almost impossible. Once through the door to the staircase, she **4.** begin ______________ to run. She reached the ground floor and **5.** walk ______________ as fast as she could across the main reception area. Then, she jumped into one of the taxis **6.** park ______________ outside the entrance.

"The nearest underground station, please. As fast as you can. I'm late for my train."

"Right you are, luv.[i] Traffic's not too bad; we might make it to Paddington 'fore three."

suspect	Verdächtigte
to groan	stöhnen

By the time Constable Rawlins reached the ground floor, there was no sign of the suspect. He groaned. He was going to be in a lot of trouble. He pulled out his mobile phone and breathed in deeply as he dialled Scotland Yard.

Auf den britischen Inseln ist es durchaus üblich, dass Fremde mit Kosenamen wie **love, sweetheart** oder **darling** angesprochen werden.

2 HALF-FORGOTTEN DREAMS

Luckily, Paddington Station was not that far away, so it only cost Esther ten pounds. She walked around the busy train station, feeling lost and wondering what to do. The station seemed familiar to her but she could not remember when she had last been there. Hungry and thirsty, she bought herself a sandwich and a small bottle of water from a station kiosk, which left her with just thirty-seven pounds in her pocket.

to knock over	umstoßen

There were lots of businessmen with briefcases rushing back and forth, mothers with excited children and young couples with rucksacks and London A-Z maps. (i)

Der Stadtplan **London A-Z** mit Spiralbindung ist ein wahrer Klassiker und ein Muss für jeden Londonbesucher.

Everyone except me knows where they are going and where they are from, Esther thought desperately as she sat on a bench and watched them. When she stood up again, she was almost knocked over by a young businessman who was running, as best he could, through the crowd.

"Silly cow! Why don't you look where you're going?" he shouted rudely as he continued running.

"Idiot," she shouted back. "Why don't you!"

Then Esther saw that the man had dropped a train timetable on the ground next to her feet. She picked it up and examined it. It was for trains to Plymouth, one of which was leaving from platform 5 in less than fifteen minutes. Tickets cost thirty-five pounds.

"Plymouth, that's far from here. Go there!" shouted the voice. "Come on, get a ticket. The police will be here soon. You have to get away."

There were long **queues** of tourists in front of the ticket counters, but there were also self-service ticket machines. She ran over to one of them and typed in the details from the timetable.

The machine seemed to take ages to process each step. Esther anxiously watched the big clock above the entrance.

"Come on," she **muttered**. "Get on with it."

"Yeah, get on with it," echoed the voice.

At last, the machine spat out the ticket. Grabbing it, Esther pushed past the queue behind her and ran towards Platform 5. She showed her ticket at the gate and walked across the platform. She feared that she would be called back at any second by someone who had recognized her – but nobody did.

"I've made it," she sighed as she sat down in a train **compartment**

"For the moment," the cruel voice replied.

queue	Warteschlange
to mutter	murren, brummeln
compartment	Abteil
exhausted	erschöpft
to dare	wagen
to lose one's temper	wütend werden, in Zorn geraten
unconscious	bewusstlos
growl	Knurren
traffic warden	Verkehrspolizist

She had no idea what she was going to do in Plymouth, but for the moment, she was happy to have a comfortable seat and to know that she could relax for a few hours. She was **exhausted**. She did not **dare** remove the beret or the dark glasses, but by the time the train had left London, she was fast asleep.

When Detective Inspector Robert Mulligan lost his temper, it was best to be as far away as possible. Constable Rawlins was glad that he was at the other end of the phone when he told the DI that Esther Radcliffe had escaped.
"What do you mean she has escaped?" Mulligan shouted. "The woman was unconscious and, as far as I know, there is only one door into her room, which YOU were guarding. Or did she manage to fly out of the window?"

Exercise 9: Odd one out. Welches Wort ist das „schwarze Schaf"? Unterstreichen Sie!

1. desperate frightened hopeless impossible
2. anxiously fearfully nervously rudely
3. briskly quickly carefully rapidly
4. taxi train platform compartment
5. stutter mutter murmur think

"Well, I'm not really sure, sir..."
Rawlins heard a deep growl and something heavy being thrown on a desk. "Unless you wish to continue your career as a traffic warden, I suggest that you have a few more answers by the time I get to the hospital. Is that CLEAR?"
"Crystal clear, sir," muttered the pale young man in the black uniform.

When Esther got off the train in Plymouth, they were waiting for her. Somebody had recognized her on the train and called the police. Six police officers pulled her away from the other passengers and pushed her face down on the ground. They roughly pulled her arms behind her and handcuffed her. They then frogmarched her to a waiting police van, in which she was then handcuffed to a rail. Everything after that happened very quickly. She was driven back to London and appeared before court almost immediately. Nobody believed her story about amnesia, although she repeated it over and over again. So she was quickly found guilty of murder and received a twenty-five year sentence. The police took her straight from court to Holloway Prison where a female guard marched her to her cell, pushed her inside and slammed the door. The only light was from the moon, which she could see through the bars of her window. She pushed her hands through the bars and screamed...

"This train will arrive at Plymouth Station in five minutes. The journey terminates there. Please make sure that you take all of your luggage with you."

Confused and still half asleep, Esther looked around her. Had it all just been a dream? Slowly the events of the past few hours came back to her.

It was beginning to get dark outside, and she felt cold. Opposite her, a man in his early thirties smiled.

to handcuff	Handschellen anlegen
to frogmarch	(im Polizeigriff) abführen
sentence	*hier*: Strafe, Strafmaß
to slam	zuknallen
bar	*hier*: Gitterstab
embarrassed	verlegen
to glance	flüchtig blicken
to find shelter	Schutz finden

"You obviously have no problems sleeping on trains," he grinned. "I got on at Bath, and you were already fast asleep then."

"I've had a hard couple of days," Esther answered, pushing her dark glasses firmly back on her nose.

The man stared at her. "Are you from Plymouth? I'm sure I've seen you somewhere before."

Esther tried to look annoyed, though she was trembling inside.

The man seemed a little embarrassed. "Well, I could be wrong, of course."
He stood up and pulled down his leather jacket and a small rucksack from the overhead luggage rack. Esther pretended to study the English countryside outside the window, while she wondered anxiously how the man had recognized her. She glanced down at the newspaper on the seat. What if there had been a photograph of her in the newspaper?
It was raining. She hoped she would find somewhere at Plymouth station where she could hide and find shelter for the night.

Exercise 10: Fill in the blanks. Lesen Sie weiter und setzen Sie folgenden Wörter in die passende Lücke ein!

space | travellers | passenger | while | copy

At Plymouth, Esther's fellow **1.** ______ left the train without saying another word. He left his **2.** ______ of The Daily Telegraph on the seat beside him, so Esther picked it up and got off the train. Not sure what to do next, she found a **3.** ______ among the **4.** ______ waiting for the 9:45 p.m. train back to London. It was 8:20 p.m., so she could sit hidden in the crowd for a **5.** ______ to think about what to do.

I've been here before, Esther thought. The station was familiar. She remembered that lots of people had been waiting for her the last time she arrived. Thankfully, not this time.
Esther felt a rush of fear. Her hands and legs were trembling uncontrollably. She knew that the old woman in the hospital had been right – if she thought for long enough, she would remember. But she also knew that she didn't have time to think – to remember. There were probably many people looking for her.
She also felt very alone. She had absolutely no money left and had no idea what to do next. And the worst thing was that she didn't even know if she really had killed someone or not.
There was nothing about the murder in the newspaper she had taken from the train, but it was a day old. The evening papers would probably include the story, and the new issue of the Telegraph would definitely cover it.

As if to confirm her thoughts, a bearded man with an Alsatian walked past. Under his arm was a copy of The Plymouth Herald. There was a big picture of Esther on the front page.
Esther stood up and walked slowly towards the exit. A copy of The Herald had been left on one of the seats, so she swapped it for The Daily Telegraph (i) and folded it with her picture on the inside.
Outside the station there were six coaches. People were milling around, trying to work out which coach was theirs.

Der **Daily Telegraph** ist eine überregionale, eher konservative Tageszeitung. Der **Plymouth Herald** ist eine lokale Boulevardzeitung. In Anlehnung an ihr jeweiliges Format werden großformatige, seriöse Zeitungen **broadsheets** und die kleineren Boulevardblätter **tabloids** genannt.

"Are you also staying at the Woods International Resort?" a rather worried-looking, elderly lady asked.
"Is that where you're staying?" Esther asked.

"Yes," the woman replied.
"What is your name?"
"Mary Watson."
"Don't you have any luggage?"
"It's been put on the coach, but I don't know which one. I'm so tired and hungry I just don't have the energy to run from bus to bus."
"Look, why don't you wait here, and I'll go and find out for you."
"Oh, that's very kind," the woman said gratefully, sitting down heavily on the nearest seat.
Esther walked past a crowd of people complaining to one of the travel agents.
"Why isn't our bus here? I've just travelled all the way from Norwich. I do not want to sit here waiting for another hour and a half."
"I'm sorry, Mr Peterson," answered the **flustered** travel operator. "The bus to the Premier Inn has broken down, and we have to wait for a replacement. I've got **vouchers** for the restaurant across the road. Why don't you go and get yourself something to eat?"
Mr Peterson and the other travellers all **surged forward**, so it was easy for Esther to **merge into** the group and to get one of the vouchers, too. At least now she would get something to eat.
The third coach in the queue was the one going to the Woods International Resort – and it was nearly full. Esther thought quickly. Should she take the coach? She could give Mrs Watson the voucher.

to cover sth.	über etw. berichten
to confirm	bestätigen
Alsatian	Deutscher Schäferhund
to swap	austauschen
coach	Reisebus
to mill around	umherlaufen
flustered	gestresst, nervös
voucher	Gutschein
to surge forward	nach vorne drängen
to merge into	in der Menge aufgehen

Exercise 11: Much or many? **Welche Mengenangabe ist hier richtig?**

1. Esther did not have ______ money left in her pocket.
2. There were ______ people waiting for the next train.
3. There were not ______ articles about the crime in the paper.
4. She didn't have ______ more time.
5. I don't like her music ______, but ______ people love it.

Hadn't the old woman said that she was hungry and tired? She could relax in the restaurant for a while… Meanwhile, Esther could go and have a shower in Mrs Watson's hotel room. Perhaps she could even find a coat or something else of use in the woman's luggage. Would it be stealing if Esther "borrowed" a few things? Anyway, she could pay Mrs Watson back when she had proved her innocence. Esther knew that she had to stay on the move. The police might already have recognized her face on one of the CCTV cameras[i] at Paddington Station – or even at Plymouth Station…

Closed Circuit Television Cameras. Diese Überwachungskameras sind im öffentlichen Raum in England allgegenwärtig und sehr umstritten.

She rushed back to Mary Watson, who had taken off one of her shoes and was rubbing her toes. She looked up when Esther walked over.
"Oh, there you are. You are so kind. Did you find out anything?"
"Yes. Unfortunately, your coach has broken down. I've got a voucher for you, so that you can go and have a meal at the restaurant opposite. The tour operator will come and call you when your coach arrives."
"Well, it could have been worse. Thank you for your help, dear."
"My pleasure," answered Esther, feeling absolutely awful.
She was turning into a real criminal, she reflected. Or was she already a criminal and she just couldn't remember? But murder...?
She turned and walked briskly over to the Woods International Resort coach.
"Name?" said the driver.
"Mary Watson," Esther answered.
The driver looked down his list and ticked off her, or rather Mrs Watson's, name. Esther went to the back of the coach and slumped down in the corner.

innocence	Unschuld
to tick off	abhaken
to slump	zusammensacken
jigsaw piece	Puzzlestück

Even Detective Inspector Mulligan took a while to work out how Esther Radcliffe had escaped. However, when her evening dress was found in the room next door and a patient with a broken leg complained loudly that someone had stolen her clothes, the jigsaw pieces began to fit together.
Mulligan was surprised – and impressed. He went out to the back courtyard to look up at the window. The ledge the singer had stood on looked very narrow from below. Anyone who dared such an escape must be desperate to get away. He lit a cigar to think about how exactly she had done it. When he realized that the demented old woman must have opened the window for Esther, he smiled.

Exercise 12: Hidden words. **Hier verstecken sich sechs Gegenstände, die man auf eine Reise mitnimmt!**

G	Z	T	T	N	W	G	M	K
F	S	W	I	M	S	U	I	T
A	U	T	C	C	O	I	D	O
N	I	K	K	F	F	D	U	V
G	T	X	E	M	Q	E	V	N
S	C	N	T	S	M	N	G	H
P	A	S	S	P	O	R	T	X
D	S	P	O	A	N	A	E	L
W	E	Q	P	L	E	Z	H	Y
B	H	K	G	E	Y	P	L	B

When the young woman told the receptionist at the Woods International Resort that she was Mrs Watson, the receptionist was immediately suspicious. Her computer told her that Mrs Watson was a pensioner (i) and a golfer. The pretty young woman in front of her was definitely neither of those. She was in her late twenties or early thirties, and judging by the red beret and dark sunglasses, she had something to hide. Only couples and groups tended to stay at the resort – which was a twenty-minute drive from Plymouth's nightlife – or golfers. Or ...

Pensioner bedeutet ganz allgemein „Rentner" und bezieht sich – anders als das deutsche „Pensionär" – nicht nur auf Personen, die im öffentlichen Dienst gearbeitet haben.

She asked the woman for some identification and noticed the confusion her question caused.

"I've left my passport in my suitcase. I'll bring it down later."

"Please do," the receptionist smiled and handed her the key for her room. "The room's on the ground floor in the east wing overlooking the garden, and your luggage should already be in the room."
"Thank you. That sounds lovely."
Esther tried to walk as naturally as she could. Yet, she could feel the trembling in her arms and legs. It was obvious that the receptionist was suspicious of her – and would probably talk to the manager. She didn't have much time.

suspicious	*hier*: misstrauisch
judging by	nach etw. zu urteilen
to long to	sich sehnen
split second	Bruchteil einer Sekunde

Exercise 13: Unscramble. Bringen Sie die Buchstaben in die richtige Reihenfolge!

1. gldee ____________________
2. etipecirostn ____________________
3. oennnecic ____________________
4. prsieneno ____________________
5. pciissusou ____________________

Mrs Watson's room was very nice. Esther longed to lie down on the comfortable bed and go to sleep. She was so tired – and still dizzy, too. However, she just couldn't allow herself the luxury of sleep.
She ate the welcome chocolate on the pillow and took some peanuts and bottled water from the minibar. For a split second, she

saw herself with a blonde man. They were sitting, eating together in a hotel room. She was very happy… But who was he? Frustration and fear instantly washed away the positive feelings. There was no time for this now. She had to find a safe place first.
Quickly, she finished the peanuts and pulled Mrs Watson's suitcase on to the bed. The lock was very small and easy to break open. Soon everything from inside the suitcase was spread over the bed. The first item Esther took was a small rucksack. In it, she put a jumper, a couple of t-shirts, an anorak, some socks, a scarf and a small torch. In a small purse at the bottom of the suitcase, she also discovered three hundred pounds, which she gratefully added to the rucksack. From the bathroom, she took a towel, the complimentary toothbrush, soap and shampoo.

item	Gegenstand
complimentary	*hier*: Gratis-, kostenlos
ϟ to jump out of one's skin	sich zu Tode erschrecken
tearful	weinerlich
ϟ Never mind!	Egal! Was soll's!

She nearly jumped out of her skin when someone knocked on the door.
"Who is it?" she called out.
A boy answered. "Mrs Watson, the receptionist asked me to remind you about the identification she needs. She is only on duty for another hour, so she asked if you would go down as soon as you can."
"I'm just about to have a shower. Tell her I will be down in half an hour."
The boy hesitated outside the door for a moment. "I could take your passport down if you wish," he called out.
"No, young man, I will bring it down myself in half an hour, as I have just said." Esther tried to sound annoyed, but in fact she just sounded tearful

Exercise 14: Adjective or adverb? **Ergänzen Sie die richtige Form!**

1. The room was luxurious ______________________________ ______________ furnished.
2. She played golf very good __________________________ ______________.
3. There was a loud _____________________________ knock on the door.
4. He had a guilty _____________________________ look on his face.
5. The hotel staff did not give up easy ________________ __________________.

Well, so much for having a shower, she sighed. Never mind. Time to leave. Grabbing some more of the peanuts and chocolate from the minibar, as well as a couple of small bottles of soft drinks, Esther closed the rucksack.

She turned the shower on. Then, for the second time that day, she made her escape through a window. It was already dark, so nobody saw her leave. And it took a while before the boy waiting outside the door realized that even a woman could not shower forever.

The receptionist called the local police at 10:00 p.m. They arrived about the same time as a rather tired and confused Mrs Watson.

Constable Rawlins was busy doing as he had been told by Mulligan. He asked everyone in the reception area of the hospital about Esther Radcliffe and then talked to every taxi driver in front of the hospital. Taxi drivers love gossip. Gossip passes the time of day when they are waiting for the next customer. Thus, word spread quickly that someone may have picked up a murderess. At the end of the day, a tired Constable Rawlins phoned DI Mulligan to tell him that Esther Radcliffe had been driven to Paddington.

gossip	Tratsch
word spread	es hat sich herumgesprochen
solitary	abgelegen, einsam
barn	Scheune
to creak	knarren
to scurry	huschen
to hoot	rufen (Eule)
to emerge	herauskommen, hervortreten

"Well done, Rawlins," Mulligan answered with a mouth full of take-away pizza. "Tomorrow, you go down to Paddington Station and pick up copies of the CCTV recordings."

Exercise 15: Choose the correct alternative. Lesen Sie weiter und unterstreichen Sie die richtige Variante!

At about the same time, Jean Jary was reading the headlines **1.** angrily / anxiously. She needed to find Esther before anyone else did. But **2.** how / who was she going to find her? Right now, she could be **3.** everywhere / anywhere. It would be very risky to show **4.** too / to much interest in finding her. They had all been in the room with Esther and Paul Tyne that evening: Rick, Andy, Sam, Susan and Bill. **5.** Somebody / Nobody had wanted to go home. They had all been having so much fun - **6.** at least / at last to start with.

The person Jean was thinking about was wandering in the moonlight along the coast of Cornwall.

Eventually, [i] Esther found a solitary barn full of fresh-smelling hay. She sensed that normally she would never have dared to sleep in such a place. Perhaps Esther – whoever she was – had been scared of spiders, mice and other small creatures. However, compared with the terror she had experienced that day, such fears seemed childish. Anyway, Esther was completely exhausted; she didn't care where she slept. She climbed up a ladder and found a comfortable spot, lay down on a couple of Mrs Watson's t-shirts and covered herself with the anorak.

Achtung false friends

eventually ≠ eventuell	
eventually	schließlich
possibly	eventuell

It did not bother her that the barn door creaked, small animals scurried along the ground beneath her or that an owl hooted on the roof. For a long time, she stared at the wooden roof above her. She thought back over the day. How strange and frightening it had all been. Even if she was not a murderess – which was not certain – she had definitely turned into a thief. What was she going to do? She felt so desolate. Eventually, though she managed to fall asleep. In her dreams, her memories began to emerge from their hiding place in her brain.

Exercise 16: True or false? Welche Aussagen sind korrekt? Markieren Sie mit richtig ✓ oder falsch –!

1. DI Mulligan is told that Esther was seen at Oxford Station. ❐
2. Jean Jary enjoyed the evening with Paul and the others. ❐
3. Esther wanted to go to another hotel. ❐
4. There were noises in the barn. ❐
5. Esther found it difficult to sleep in the barn. ❐

3 BAND ON THE RUN

On Friday, Detective Inspector Mulligan asked the members of The Ballads and Balladies band as well as the make-up artist and technician to come down to the station to make a statement. It had not been difficult to arrange a meeting since without their lead singer, the band had had to cancel its tour.

to make a statement	eine Aussage machen
to scowl	finster blicken

The group arrived together in the band's bus. When told that each one of them would be called in separately to make a statement, they were not happy.

"Why's that then?" asked the drummer Richard Marks rather aggressively. "We've all come down together. Are we supposed to wait around outside until everyone is allowed to go? Why can't we just answer the questions together? We were all there at the time."

DI Mulligan stared at the skinny young man in blue jeans and an Isle of Wight Festival[i] t-shirt for a moment before answering: "You were all in the same place but will not all have experienced the same thing. It is important that we get as much detail as possible. Of course, it is also a way of checking that you are telling the truth." This neither seemed to impress nor frighten the drummer. He simply scowled and put his hands in his pockets.

Das jährliche Isle of Wight Musik-Festival auf der gleichnamigen Insel vor der Südküste Englands ist weltberühmt – es gilt als das „europäische Woodstock".

Mulligan pretended to be picking up some papers as he examined the other people in the room. Years of practice meant that he had an excellent memory for names and faces. There were five people in the room: Andrew Button was the oldest member of the band at 32. He was a good-looking, likeable sort of guy and was said to be one of the best guitarists in England. Sam Silver, the pianist, was a quiet, round-shouldered character, who rarely said anything but was well worth listening to when he did. Susan, the backing vocalist, was an attractive blonde, while the other woman, make-up artist Jean Jary, was rather plain and quite plump. And the gorilla-sized man in the corner was Bill Perez, who was a bit of an all-rounder.

backing vocalist	Backgroundsängerin
plump	pummelig
to commit sth.	etw. begehen
to frame sb.	jdm. etw. anhängen
nasty	*hier*: unangenehm
to charge	*hier*: anklagen

"Are you sure that Esther committed the murder? Perhaps she's been framed," Jean Jary commented suddenly.

There was a nasty silence.

Mulligan waited for one of them to say something, but they didn't.

"There are a number of facts that seem to indicate that Esther Radcliffe is guilty of the murder," Mulligan eventually answered. "Why else would she have run away from the hospital? Nobody had charged her with murder at the time, so she is running away from something she knows about – or at least so it would seem. The amount of drugs she swallowed seems to indicate that she wanted to kill herself. The doctor has confirmed that she nearly succeeded, too. It was only thanks to the chambermaid she was found in time."

Again the loud silence. What weren't they telling him?

"Mr Marks, why don't you come through with me first. Detective Sergeant Dawson will stay with the rest of you here. I assure you that the procedure will not take too long."

Mulligan stared slightly impatiently at Dawson, whose eyes had not left Susan Ellington's fishnet stockings since she walked in.

Exercise 17: Simple past or present perfect. Setzen Sie bitte die richtige Verbform ein!

1. DI Mulligan interview ______________________ the band members yesterday.
2. She escape ______________________ through the window 10 minutes ago.
3. "I never be ______________________ to Plymouth," she said.
4. They not sell ______________________ very many albums last year.
5. The band members know ______________________ each other since they were at school.

Esther sat up quickly, wondering how long she had been asleep. She peered down at the ground below her. No one. Then she scanned the area outside the barn through holes in the wooden planks of the walls. No one. Just as she was about to lie down again, there was a sudden movement behind her. Started, she screamed out loud. Swinging round, she was just in time to see a little brown mouse running for its life. For the first time in what seemed a lifetime, she relaxed slightly.

"I know how you feel," she murmured, watching the terrified mouse disappear.
For a while, she dozed, and as she did so, her memory slowly began to return. It seemed to be in the process of putting itself into chronological order. At the moment, like an old lady, her clearest memories were of her childhood. She remembered trips with her mother and father to the beach.
"Mum, Dad. How could I forget you, even for a minute?" Esther said out loud.
Despite the sense of terror that didn't leave her for a minute, she was beginning to feel a bit stronger. Every time she fitted another piece of the broken jigsaw in her mind she felt less alone, less helpless – although there were still many pieces to go.
Outside, it was raining quite heavily now, so she decided to stay in the barn for a bit longer. Resting really did help her mind, it seemed. She dozed again. She remembered how often she had walked across the Tunbridge Wells common in the rain with her family and their Labrador Max. And how often she had been caught in the rain when riding her bike to school. She had not been particularly bright at school. The teachers had encouraged her to focus on her one big talent: music.

common	*hier*: Gemeindeland
dread	Furcht, Grauen
to carve	schnitzen
supporting beam	Stützbalken

Esther knew that music had been one of the most important things in her life. At the same time, she could still not remember any of the songs she sang. The nurses had said that they were love songs.
Suddenly, tears of frustration started running down her cheeks. She was not going to move until she remembered at least one song. For a few minutes nothing happened. She listened to the rain hitting the barn roof. The dread of being discovered came back.

I can't lie here all day trying to remember songs, she said to herself. Was she mad? Perhaps they had already found out where she was. She sat up and took deep breaths to try and calm herself. Suddenly, another key to her mind appeared in the dark. A heart had been roughly carved into a supporting beam near her head. Next to it were two names: Shirley and Barry.

For a few moments, all the other creatures in the barn stood still and listened, as a beautiful voice rang out with a few verses of an old Shirley Bassey song:

"Livin' alone
I think of all the friends I've known
When I dial the telephone
Nobody's home
All by myself
Don't wanna be
All by myself
Anymore!"

Exercise 18: Correcting slang. Wie lautet die korrekte Schreibweise der markierten umgangssprachlichen Wendungen?

1. I don't **wanna** be by myself. ______________________
2. You **gotta** help me. ______________________
3. I **ain't** got **nobody.** ______________________
4. I **dunno.** ______________________
5. **Gotcha!** ______________________

Constable Rawlins had put his foot in it again. Detective Inspector Mulligan was furious. The last members of Esther Radcliffe's group had just left. Mulligan's face immediately took on a very unhealthy red colour. Everyone in the front office was silent. They knew when trouble was brewing: when Mulligan's eyebrows met in the middle to form a long, thick black line. With an angry jerk of his head, the DI made it quite clear to Rawlins that he was to follow him to his office.

↯ to put one's foot in it	ins Fettnäpfchen treten
furious	wütend
↯ Trouble was brewing.	Es herrschte dicke Luft.
jerk	Ruck, Zuckung

As soon as Rawlins closed the door, he exploded.

Exercise 19: Prefixes. Bilden Sie das Gegenteil der Begriffe mit den Vorsilben ir-, dis-, in-, im-, non- und un-!

1. healthy ____________________
2. tolerant ____________________
3. regular ____________________
4. polite ____________________
5. honest ____________________
6. smoker ____________________

"What the hell is the matter with you? Have you gone mad, or are you just stupid? How dare you burst into the office and inform EVERYONE that Esther Radcliffe took the train to Plymouth. The people sitting with Detective Dawson are all directly connected with the case. What if one of them was actually involved in the crime?"

Achtung false friends		
actually	≠	aktuell
actually		tatsächlich
currently		aktuell

"I'm sorry, sir," stuttered Rawlins. "I didn't think... I was just so excited to have recognized Esther Radcliffe on the CCTV camera as she got onto the train. I..."

Mulligan stood up and threw his pen at the young policeman. "Get OUT, NOW! I don't want to see your face again today."

When Rawlins had left the office, Mulligan opened the drawer next to his desk and took out a bottle of whisky and a glass. He unscrewed the top and poured himself a generous amount of the amber liquid, which he always drank neat.

He stood up and walked to the window. Instead of staring down at the busy London road, as he usually did, he found himself examining his own reflection. The years of murder cases had taken their toll. His eyelids were dark and heavy from many sleepless nights; his thick, greying eyebrows and the hard lines around his mouth showed not only how tough he had become but also, as he admitted himself, a growing intolerance. He was just getting too old for this job, he reflected. He no longer found murder investigations "exciting", like young Rawlins. He even found the murderers predictable nowadays, although...

case	*hier*: Fall
amber	bernsteinfarben
neat	*hier*: pur
to take its toll	Tribut fordern
investigation	Ermittlung
predictable	berechenbar
account	*hier*: Bericht

He walked back to his desk and opened the folder with the band's statements. They had all given a similar account of the evening. After the successful concert, everyone – except for Andrew Button, who was feeling a bit sick – had met up in Paul Tyne's suite at the

Wellington Arms Hotel to celebrate. Esther had got very drunk, which Sam Silver and Jean Jary said was unusual because she did not normally drink much. When the others decided to go home, Esther was dozing on the couch. Paul Tyne told the others to leave Esther where she was to sleep it off. Everyone else had gone home.

Exercise 20: Prepositions. Lesen Sie weiter und ergänzen Sie den Text mit den richtigen Präpositionen!

The murder took place at about half 1. ________ one in the morning. It was not 2. ________ eight o'clock the following morning that the chambermaid had found the two of them. Paul Tyne had been killed with a heavy lamp. The "murder weapon" was found next 3. ________ an unconscious Esther. She had blood 4. ________ her hands and on her dress. And she was still holding the glass of water with which she had taken the cocktail of pills – some 5. ________ which were found next to the body.

Nonetheless, there was something about this case which awakened the younger self in Mulligan. It was somehow intriguing. Something didn't quite add up. And he was determined to find out what it was.

Esther was soaked to the skin. She had walked across miles[i] and miles of fields, avoiding the roads and any villages. She still jumped every time she heard a car in the distance. It was frightening walking across the open countryside. She felt very vulnerable. Eventually, she found herself walking along a path overlooking an estuary. About a mile away, she could see a medium-sized town and started to walk towards it. She began to meet people walking their dogs. It was still quite windy, so she was able to keep the hood of her anorak up without it seeming strange. When people greeted her, she returned the greeting. Otherwise, she kept her eyes firmly on the ground every time she went past someone.

Briten lieben ihre Traditionen und verwenden daher trotz der Umstellung auf das Dezimalsystem noch immer sehr gern die Längenmaße **miles, feet** und **inches** sowie die Gewichte **stones, pounds** und **ounces.**

As she approached the beach road, she heard a mother calling her son, "Tristan, hurry up! We're going to miss the bus to Saltash. The next one isn't for two hours."

The bus was waiting in the car park next to the beach. It was relatively full, so nobody paid any attention to her. She put her wet rucksack on the seat next to her, hoping that it would stop anyone from wanting to use the empty seat. Then she remembered the newspaper she had picked up at Plymouth Station. She pulled it out of the rucksack to read the article.

to sleep it off	einen Rausch ausschlafen
nonetheless	nichtsdestotrotz
intriguing	faszinierend
ϟ to add up	*hier*: Sinn ergeben, stimmen
determined	entschlossen
soaked to the skin	klatschnass
to jump	*hier*: zusammenzucken
vulnerable	verwundbar
estuary	(Fluss-)Mündung, Meeresarm

Rising Star Murders Agent

Last night, Esther Radcliffe (29), who became known with her band The Ballads and Balladies for their song "Love is like a Ripple in the Ocean", was found unconscious next to the body of her murdered agent, Paul Tyne, in his suite at the Wellington Arms. Radcliffe, who has just completed a very successful concert tour, is thought to have killed her agent while under the influence of alcohol and drugs. At the moment, little is known about the exact circumstances of the crime.

"As far as I know, Paul and Esther had not had a fight recently," commented backing vocalist Susan Ellington.

The singer is currently under police surveillance at a London hospital and has not yet been officially charged with the murder.

Esther looked at the picture on the front page. It showed her with the other members of the band. She recognized the faces, and slowly the names came back to her: Rick, Sam, Susan and Andy. Suddenly she realized that Andy was the man she had remembered yesterday in the hotel room. It hit her like a thunderbolt. He was the man she loved…, wasn't he?

Her thoughts were interrupted as the bus arrived in Saltash. She put the newspaper away and got off the bus. For a while, Esther wandered around like a tourist, staring distractedly at the Union Jack Inn, the famous Royal Albert Railway Bridge and Trematon Castle in the distance. But after a while, she awoke as if from a trance. What was she doing? Someone might recognize her. She had

ripple	kleine Welle, Plätschern
under police surveillance	polizeilich überwacht
thunderbolt	Blitzschlag
distractedly	zerstreut, unkonzentriert
appearance	Aussehen
auburn	rotbraun
donation	Spende
newsstand	Zeitungskiosk
exposed	exponiert, schutzlos

to think of a plan. First of all, she needed to change her appearance On seeing a Boots Chemist, she went inside and bought herself some auburn hair colour, some make-up and a new pair of sunglasses.

Exercise 21: Simple past or past perfect. Setzen Sie die richtige Verbform ein!

1. Esther had some money that Mrs Anderson (give) ____________ her.
2. She was walking along the platform when she (see) ____________ a woman fall.
3. Esther did not know Mrs Watson. She (never see) ____________ her before.
4. Esther was hungry, so she (go) ____________ to buy a sandwich.

Outside the shop, a man walked straight up to her. Esther froze. "Oh sorry, dear. I didn't mean to give you a fright. I'm collecting for the Red Cross. Would you like to make a small donation?"
Nodding nervously, Esther put a pound coin in the collection box. "Thanks a lot, dear," said the man, turning away immediately to catch another woman just going past.
Esther had thought that she would feel safer in the town. After half an hour of avoiding every direct glance, crossing the street twice because she saw a policeman and three times because she saw a newsstand, she was feeling more exposed than ever. She continu-

ously turned round to make sure nobody was following her. She had to find somewhere to stay or rather hide. She started walking up and down the side streets in search of accommodation.
Most of the bed and breakfasts had "no vacancies" signs hanging outside, but one rather run-down building had a "room to let" sign. She knocked on the door, and a young girl in a pink dress opened it.

Exercise 22: Fill in the blanks. Lesen Sie weiter und ergänzen Sie mit dem richtigen Wort!

"Mum, there's someone here for the room," the girl shouted. A young 1. ______, hardly more than a child herself, came running out of the kitchen, a screaming toddler under her arm.

"Please do come 2. ______," she smiled. "How long do you want to 3. ______?"

"How much does the room 4. ______?" Esther asked warily

"Thirty-five pounds per day," the woman answered. "I can give you a key, so you can come and go when you like. I'm afraid I don't serve 5. ______, though. I've got six children, so there is enough going on in my kitchen in the morning."

"That's fine with me," answered Esther. "I don't normally eat breakfast."

The woman was obviously relieved.

"There is a kitchenette with one hotplate, a small fridge, a kettle, saucepans, cups, cutlery and so on."

Three boys suddenly came noisily down the stairs.

"Wow, is she going to stay here?" asked a ginger-haired Indian with no front teeth.

"Not if you horrors carry on making such a racket," his mother joked, looking at Esther nervously.

The little girl in the pink dress pulled Esther's jacket. "Why are you wearing dark glasses and an old-lady scarf?"

"Lizzie!" her mother exclaimed angrily.

It was unlikely that this mother of six had much time to follow what was going on in the rest of the world, Esther reflected. The woman interrupted her thoughts.

"Do you still want to see the room?"

"Yes, please, Mrs...?" answered Esther.

The woman's mouth opened slightly in surprise. "Tarbitt." She turned towards the narrow staircase. "It's on the top floor. There is a staircase up the other side of the house, so you actually have your own entrance. There isn't a television, but my last tenant left an old laptop in the room, so you have Internet access."

Esther knew that she was going to accept the room, even before she had seen it.

accommodation	Unterkunft
run-down	heruntergekommen
toddler	Kleinkind
warily	vorsichtig, misstrauisch
kitchenette	Kochnische
hotplate	Kochplatte
cutlery	Besteck
ginger-haired	rothaarig
⚡ to make a racket	Krawall machen
tenant	Mieter

Exercise 23: Word spiral. **Finden Sie die Begriffe in der Wortspirale!**

1	2	3	4	5	6	7
22	23	24	25	26	27	8
21	36	37	38	39	28	9
20	35	42	41	40	29	10
19	34	33	32	31	30	11
18	17	16	15	14	13	12

1–7: The name of the town where Esther decides to stay.

7–13: Mrs Tarbitt calls her children…

13–19: Esther is the main … in a murder case.

19–21: The flat is on the … floor.

21–26: Lizzie asks a rude question. She is not …

26–32: Esther arrived in Plymouth in the …

32–34: A murder weapon not used in this case.

34–39: The job of Beth and Susie

39–42: Children on the beach make castles out of this.

About an hour after Detective Inspector[i] Mulligan had thrown Rawlins out of his office, there was a knock on the door. Detective Sergeant Peter Dawson walked in. He had worked with Mulligan for over twenty-five years and was the only person at Scotland Yard who called him by his first name. He grinned when he saw the whisky.

"So Robert, been having a bit of trouble with young Rawlins again, I hear," he said, sitting down in the seat opposite Mulligan.

"I thought you said he was one of the best in his year," Mulligan grumbled, taking out a second glass from the drawer and putting it in front of his partner."

ϟ lad	Bursche
keen	eifrig

Titel und Berufsbezeichnungen wie **Inspector** werden im Englischen großgeschrieben, wenn es sich um eine direkte Anrede handelt oder sie als Teil eines Namens verwendet werden, z. B. **Detective Inspector Mulligan.** In allen anderen Fällen werden sie kleingeschrieben.

"He was and still is," replied Dawson patiently. "Give the lad a chance. He's only 19. He's very keen. Yes, he makes stupid mistakes, but I personally think he still has the potential to make a good police officer."

"Hmm..." Mulligan grunted. "Well, just keep him out of my way for a while if you can. Anyway, I'm sure you haven't come to talk about Rawlins. What have you got for me?"

"Esther Radcliffe did take the train all the way to Plymouth." Dawson put a faxed copy of a CCTV camera on Mulligan's desk. Esther Radcliffe was circled in red, sitting among a group of people and reading a newspaper.

Mulligan was relieved. If she had got off at one of the earlier stops, that would have made the search far more difficult.

"Have you informed the local police?"

"Yes, of course."

"Good."

"There is something else, though," Dawson continued.

"Yes?"

Exercise 24: Fill in the blanks. **Lesen Sie weiter und setzen Sie die angegebenen Wörter ein!**

committed | pathologist | weighs | hair | file | drugs

Dawson ran his hand through his **1.** ______________ . "The **2.** ______________ says that Paul Tyne was hit with such force, it seems unlikely that Esther Radcliffe could have **3.** ______________ the crime on her own. The lamp itself **4.** ______________ twenty kilos. What is more, the **5.** ______________ found on the floor are not the same as the ones found in Esther Radcliffe's blood."

"Oh hell," **swore** Mulligan and picked up the Radcliffe **6.** ______________ again.

Meanwhile, a solitary driver pulled off the motorway to answer his mobile. The voice at the other end of the line sounded panicked.
"We've got to find her."
"Yes, but how?"
"I don't know!" The mobile line went dead.
The motorway was busy, but it would still be possible to get to Plymouth before dark. But then what? thought the driver.

to swear	*hier*: fluchen

4 GHOSTS FROM THE PAST

Since the visit to the police station on Friday, they had all been avoiding one another. It was Andy who had said that the band should meet in the studio on Monday. Yet they had been there for almost an hour and hardly said a word to one another, let alone play any music. Susan had not sung anything, Rick had not tuned the drums, and Andy's guitar was still in its case. Even Sam, who was sitting at the piano, had not touched the keys.

Instead, Bill gave a monologue on the latest football results in the European Cup. He only stopped talking when Andy said that he needed to cancel the concert at Marco's.

let alone	ganz zu schweigen
to tune	(Instrument) stimmen
keys *pl*	*hier*: Tasten
teeny weeny	klitzeklein
stubbornly	hartnäckig, stur

Susan watched Andy put down the receiver. "I don't know why we had to cancel the gig," she grumbled. An ugly, dark shadow crossed Andrew's handsome face.

"How about the teeny weeny little problem of not having a lead singer at the moment?" he asked sarcastically. "Or the fact that our agent has just been murdered?"

"Well, we need to start working again soon," Susan said stubbornly, examining her long fingernails. "We can't just cancel everything."

Andy sighed. "I'm not cancelling everything, but I do think that we need to take a month or so off to work out where we go from here. Anyway, nobody knows for sure that Esther really is guilty of the murder. Perhaps she will be able to come back."

nastily	garstig, fies
And pigs might fly!	Wer's glaubt, wird selig.
vote of confidence	Vertrauensbeweis
to snap	blaffen
service	*hier*: Gottesdienst
appropriate	angemessen, passend
to breathe a sigh of relief	erleichtert aufatmen
aimlessly	ziellos

"Yeah right!" laughed Rick nastily, who was lying on the old studio sofa. "And pigs might fly! Sue's right. We need to talk properly. For example, who is going to speak at Paul's funeral tomorrow?"

"Rick's right, Andy," Sam commented, swinging round on the piano stool. "Naturally, we are still all in shock, but we really do need to think about what we are going to do. I spent most of the weekend lying in bed thinking, and I still have no ideas. Esther was the heart of the band. With her gone, it may not be possible to continue..."

"Thanks for the vote of confidence," Susan snapped impatiently.

Jean stood up. "I'm going to make some coffee. Let's sit around the kitchen table and talk about things sensibly. And by the way, I think Sam should speak at the service tomorrow. Will you, Sam?"

Achtung false friends

sensible	≠	sensibel
sensible		vernünftig
sensitive		sensibel

Before anyone could object, Jean continued. "Sam knew Paul long before any of us met him." She looked directly at Sam. "Weren't you even at school with him? You've been best friends for years. It really would be more appropriate if you spoke, especially as you know his parents."

Hesitantly, Sam nodded. Everyone else secretly breathed a sigh of relief. At least that was decided.

Exercise 25: If-clauses. Formen Sie die folgenden Sätze um wie im Beispiel!

1. Example: I am not a rich rock singer, so I can't buy a sports car.

   If I were a rich rock singer, I would buy a sports car.

2. I do not have a good voice, so I do not sing.

   ____

3. We don't have a lead singer, so we're not going to perform at Marco's.

   ____

4. I don't know his parents, so I'm not speaking at his funeral.

   ____

5. They are all in shock, so they don't know what to do.

   ____

"Did you find anything out while you were in Plymouth?" Jean whispered to Bill. The others were still in the kitchen drinking coffee. "No," Bill sighed. "I spent most of the day driving aimlessly around the town, hoping I would see her somewhere."

"I thought you were going to wear your old policeman's uniform?"
"I didn't dare," Bill replied. "There were too many real policemen wandering around – and the uniform has changed (i) anyway since I was in the force."

Die neue, vollkommen schwarze Polizeiuniform ist in England nicht unumstritten. Viele trauern der alten Uniform mit weißem Hemd und Krawatte hinterher.

"Do the people there know that she is in the area?"
"I don't think so. There are no pictures of her anywhere. Scotland Yard probably don't want her to know that they have worked out where she is. Otherwise, she will start moving again."
"And do you think that she is still there?"
Jean asked, dunking another ginger biscuit in her cup.
"How the hell am I supposed to know, woman!"

"Hey, aren't you Esther Radcliffe?"
Esther felt someone take her right arm and turned round quickly to find herself face to face with a thug with a broken nose.
"Let go of me immediately!" she shouted, trying to get behind her shopping trolley.
The man tightened his hold even more.
"Rob," he shouted. "Come over here. I think I've found that singer murderer."
Rob, a Neanderthal with a wide mouth, wandered over from the alcoholic drinks section, a bottle of cheap vodka in his hand. Smiling a bit like a dog about to be given a bone, he reached out to grab her left arm...

the force	(Polizei-) Truppe
to dunk	eintunken
thug	Schläger
shopping trolley	Einkaufswagen
to tighten	*hier*: fester halten, verstärken
to recur	sich wiederholen
crate	Kiste

"What do you think you are doing?" shouted Esther, trying to free her arm from his grip. "Who DO YOU think you are?"
"The question is not who WE are," shouted the gorilla. "It's who YOU are!"
He pulled on her arm, and Esther felt herself falling… again.

Exercise 26: Choose the correct alternative. Lesen Sie weiter und unterstreichen Sie die richtige Variante!

It was the second time that Esther **1.** had fallen / was falling out of bed that night. The nightmares were **2.** growing / getting worse. As soon as she went to sleep, they came back, often full of people she **3.** hasn't known / didn't know, but also with people she did know but could not place. None of them were **4.** as bad as / so bad as the recurring one of her in a prison cell. That one was really terrifying. In **5.** comparison / comparing, the one in the supermarket was almost funny. Not that she really felt like laughing.

Esther got up and walked over to the small fridge. It was full of the groceries that she had indeed bought at the small supermarket on Saturday. The two men in her dream had also been in the shop at the time. However, they had been far too busy deciding whose turn it was to pay for the crate of beer to notice – or recognize – her.
It was now eight o'clock in the morning. Esther walked over to the computer and switched it on. She had spent most of the weekend

in the room sleeping or resting, and gradually putting together the pieces in her mind. Now, she could remember most people's faces and names as well as most events from her past, but a lot of detail was still missing. Her mind was like a canvas on which the artist had painted in the outlines of the main figures, but not their features.

The worst thing was that, although she could feel her own fear, she couldn't feel any emotions towards other people – as if she were frozen. Although she knew that she had been with the band for five years and that they had had a lot of fun together, she could not recall what she had felt for them. Not even for Andy, the guitarist, with whom she obviously had (or had had?) a relationship. She remembered those funny little, intimate details that make us love the people we do, but she didn't remember loving him for them – how he hated anybody touching his guitar, his almost drug-like addiction to Red Bull and his love for his TR6 sports car.

canvas	Leinwand
addiction	Sucht, Abhängigkeit
to jog sb.'s memory	jds. Gedächtnis nachhelfen
prime suspect	Hauptverdächtige
to call in sick	sich krank melden

Esther sat down at the computer and thought for a few minutes. She had located her e-mail account and all her e-mail addresses. The only problem was that her dislike of e-mailing (which she did remember) meant that there were no personal e-mails of any kind to help jog her memory about her friends.

She sat staring at the mail that she had written the night before:

```
Hi, it's me! I'm sorry I haven't
contacted you before. I woke up on
Thursday in hospital, and at first, I
could not even remember my name, let
```

alone yours. Then I discovered that I was the **prime suspect** in a murder case. I was confused and frightened, so I decided to run. My memory is slowly coming back, but I still have no idea if I committed the murder or not. Do you know what happened? Can you help me?

Hopefully, Esther.

Esther sat staring at the mail for ages before she pressed "send" and watched it disappear on the Internet highway. Even then, she still was not sure if she had chosen the right person to send it to.

Monday morning had started out badly for DI Mulligan. The coffee machine had not been working, his secretary had called in sick and the garage had told him that it was going to cost him four hundred pounds to repair his wife's car. Added to that the fact that no progress had been made on the Radcliffe case… Mulligan was not in a good mood.
"And this is all the Plymouth police have sent?" he asked again, holding up a single sheet of faxed paper.
"Yes," answered Dawson.
"She can't just have disappeared into thin air. Someone must have seen her. How did the hotel search go?"
"We are still waiting. The police sent round a mail to all the hotels and bed and breakfast accommodations in Plymouth."
Mulligan sighed. "Well, with her photo in every major newspaper, she is unlikely to visit any public places. She'll probably be avoiding train stations, too. And she can't have much money left, either."

Exercise 27: Fill in the blanks. Setzen Sie das passende Wort ein!

1. Esther keeps falling out of bed because of her ____________________.

2. Esther was exhausted, so she spent the weekend ____________________.

3. ____________________, her memory was coming back, piece by piece.

4. There were very few personal mails to help Esther because of her intense ____________________ of e-mailing.

5. Esther didn't know who she was; she was very ____________________.

Mulligan walked over to the map of England hanging on the wall. "That means that she can't be that far from Plymouth. Could you phone Plymouth station and tell them to expand the radius of the search by another thirty miles. She's probably lying low, trying to work out what to do."

ϟ to lie low	untertauchen
to impersonate sb.	sich als jmd. ausgeben

The phone rang on Mulligan's desk. He picked it up.
"Detective Inspector Mulligan, hello!"

"Good morning, sir. This is PC Duncan from Plymouth."
Mulligan felt optimistic. "Plymouth...? Oh good, have you got something for me?"
"Yes. I'm pretty sure that the woman you are looking for is the same woman that impersonated a Mrs Watson at the Woods International Resort on Thursday."
"Thursday!" shouted Mulligan. "So why am I only hearing about it now?"

Exercise 28: Translation. Lesen Sie weiter und fügen Sie die Übersetzung der angegebenen Wörter ein. Wenn nötig, konjugieren Sie sie!

When Susan saw the e-mail from Esther, she was 1. überrascht ______________, to say the least. Rick had been standing next to Susan as she was opening her mails, so they had read the mail 2. zusammen ______________.
"What on earth shall we do?" Susan asked, turning to Rick, who was 3. offensichtlich ______________ in shock. "I 4. annehmen ______________ we should call the police."
Rick thought for a second. "No. I think we should 5. wahrscheinlich ______________ go and find her before the police do."

"Yes," Susan agreed, trying to look calm. "But it will look strange if we don't turn up to the funeral tomorrow."
"Oh shit," Rick swore, "I'd almost forgotten about that. What time does the service begin at the church?"
"11:00 a.m. And we'll have to go to the hotel afterwards, if only for an hour or so. It will be expected."
"Then I'll drive down to Plymouth straight afterwards. Send her an answer and give her my mobile number. Esther should call ME. It's a bit strange that she contacted you instead of Sam, isn't it?"

inconvenient	ungünstig, ungelegen
whereabouts	Verbleib, Aufenthaltsort
to pour in	*hier*: nach und nach eintreffen
to launch into sth.	zu etw. ansetzen, sich auf etw. stürzen
to shudder	schaudern

Susan shrugged her shoulders. Richard's mobile phone rang, and he walked across the room to pick it up.
Susan was scared. What should she do? She could not trust Rick. She had to think quickly. She read Esther's text again and then answered:

My dear Esther,
I've been so worried. I know exactly what happened. We have to be careful, though, because a lot of people are looking for you. Please do not trust anyone or talk to anyone. It's probably safer to speak on the phone than to send each other mails. Try and reach me on my mobile - 07488 927964 - tomorrow afternoon after 2:00 p.m.

Love, Susan.

She quickly pressed "send" and then closed her e-mail account just as Rick walked back.
"Have you sent a mail?"
"Yes."
"Good. I don't think that we should talk to anyone else about this, okay?"
"Okay...," Susan nodded nervously.

DI Mulligan was surprised when Jean Jary turned up at Scotland Yard later that morning. She arrived at an inconvenient time.
With the information from PC Duncan, Mulligan had managed to piece together Esther's whereabouts. He wanted to travel down to Plymouth himself, but he still had to sort out the rest of the material that was pouring in. He hoped the interruption was worth it.
"Good morning, Ms Jary. It's a surprise to see you here again so soon."
Almost immediately, she launched into a prepared but nervous speech. "Detective, I am almost positive that one of the band had something to do with the murder – but that person was not Esther."
"And how can you be sure of that?"
"I was just outside the door when 'it' happened," she answered.
Mulligan frowned and examined his notes. "There is no mention of this in your statement."
"I was scared," Jean almost whispered. "I heard the lamp crashing down on Paul's head...," here Jean shuddered, "and I was frightened. I thought the murderers might follow me."
Mulligan stared at the woman's moon-shaped face for a moment. It was impossible to know if she was telling the truth. Was she just trying to help Esther? Was she covering for somebody else? Or was she perhaps the murderer herself?
Mulligan took a sip of cold coffee. It was important to remain cool.
"Murderers?"

Exercise 29: Crossword puzzle. Lösen Sie das Kreuzworträtsel!

Across

2. The surname of Mulligan's partner.
5. Esther is the prime ... in this case.
6. The band decides to ... in the studio.
8. Richard's nickname
10. Andrew Button's car is a _ _ 6.
11. ... and gentlemen

Down

1. Make-up for the mouth
3. Mrs Tarbitt doesn't know Esther's dark ...
4. Andy plays this instrument.
6. Esther doesn't know if she committed the ...
7. Esther got to Plymouth by ...
9. In Esther's worst nightmare, she is locked in a ...

"What makes you so sure Esther was not involved?" Mulligan asked.
"Paul and Esther were engaged to get married."
Mulligan jolted upright in his chair. "Engaged? But I thought Esther Radcliffe was going out with Andrew Button."
"Their relationship finished ages ago, but they never told the press, because a romance between the lead singer and the guitarist gave their love songs a certain something – and added to their success."

engaged	*hier*: verlobt
to jolt upright	hochschnellen
wryly	ironisch, schief
to dye	färben
to give one-self up	sich (der Poli-zei) stellen

"And do you think it's possible that Esther and Paul might have had an argument?" he asked.
"Yes, but unlikely!"
"Why?"
Jean smiled wryly. "I'm her make-up artist. We are like hairdressers. We know everything about our clients."
But I don't know anything about you, Mulligan reflected, as he stared at the thick, mask-like make-up of the woman in front of him. He certainly did not trust her.

Esther had dyed her hair, changed her make-up and bought some clothes that she would not normally be seen dead in. She looked at the result in the mirror. A complete stranger smiled back at her. She was pretty sure that even her mother would have to look at her twice to recognize her.
She had briefly considered phoning her family, but then given up on the idea. As model citizens, her mother and father would only advise her to give herself up and prove her innocence through the courts. As even Esther was not sure whether or not she was the murderer, going to the police was not yet a helpful option.

Exercise 30: Past continuous. **Bilden Sie Sätze mit der Verlaufsform im Simple Past!**

1. Mulligan drank a cup of coffee. Jean Jary walked in.
   Mulligan was drinking a cup of coffee when Jean Jary walked in.
2. Dawson made a phone call. PC Rawlins dropped a glass.
   ____
3. Paul spoke to Esther. The murderer hit him with a lamp.
   ____
4. Mulligan drove to work. His car broke down.
   ____
5. Mulligan thought about the case. Jean Jary interrupted him.
   ____

It was 5:00 p.m. There would be a lot of people on the streets, so Esther decided to use the opportunity to get some fresh air – she could disappear in the crowd.
In summer, there were so many tourists in Saltash that nobody took much notice of Esther. She was just another one of the many thousands of visitors that the town welcomed each year.
Esther wandered along the picturesque river for an hour. People were fishing or out walking their dogs, and young couples were sit-

ting on benches or playing with their children. Life seemed so normal that Esther momentarily forgot about her problems.
As she walked back to her accommodation, however, she saw a man coming out of a shop with a lamp.
In her mind's eye, Esther suddenly saw a heavy lamp being lifted up by a man whose back was turned towards her. She was on a sofa, and she tried to stand up. Someone had pushed her back, laughing. It was a horrible, triumphant laugh. Hardly able to keep her eyes open, she had screamed. A man called out to her. He was shouting that he loved her and that he would always love her. There was fear in his voice, and then there was a terrifying **thud**. Esther's heart called out to him.
A scream. Another thud. Silence. Then there was darkness.
Luckily, everyone in the high street was far too busy going about their own business to notice the pretty young woman in a flowery dress with tears running down her face.

picturesque	malerisch
in her mind's eye	vor ihrem geistigen Auge
thud	dumpfer Aufschlag

Exercise 31: Idioms with heart. Welche Redewendung passt zur Frage bzw. Aussage? Kreuzen Sie an!

1. Can you always tell how she is feeling?

a) ☐ Does she always have her heart in the right place?

b) ☐ Does she always wear her heart on her sleeve?

c) ☐ Does she always put her hand on her heart?

2. She is such a kind and generous woman.

a) ❒ She has a heart of stone.

b) ❒ She has a heart of oak.

c) ❒ She has a heart of gold.

3. Esther felt a moment of great fear.

a) ❒ Her heart was in her mouth.

b) ❒ She had heart failure.

c) ❒ She was sick at heart.

5 ABSENT FRIENDS

It rained, which seemed appropriate for a funeral. The service took place at a small church in Tonbridge in Kent and all the pews were full. Susan, Rick, Andy, Sam, Jean and Bill sat at the back of the church. Many heads turned in their direction both during the service and afterwards at the reception.

In fairness, Paul's family were extremely gracious and spoke with each member of the band. As the family knew about Paul's engagement, none of them could believe that Esther was guilty.

However, the family was obviously alone in thinking this, and as the whispering gradually grew louder, the band members made their escape.

pew	Kirchenbank
gracious	*hier*: liebenswürdig
squashed	gequetscht
to hiss	zischen
to retort	scharf erwidern

"It was a nice service. Does that sound a bit strange?" remarked Bill as they all sat squashed in the bus on the way back to the studio.

"Yes," Sam agreed. "It was good to see so many people there."

"Did you notice how everyone stared at us, though?" Susan hissed. "Just because we were Esther's friends."

"Some of us at least," Sam retorted. "Anyway, it's not really that surprising. We were all in the room shortly before Paul was murdered. It could have been one of us, for all they know."

Susan **glared at** Sam angrily. "And sweet little Esther is not capable of such a thing, of course! I don't think you know Esther very well."
"I think I do," replied Sam quietly. "And I also know that you two did not **get on**. So save your crocodile tears for the press. You're **delighted** she's no longer around. You're probably already planning to take her place."

Exercise 32: True or false? **Welche Aussagen sind korrekt? Markieren Sie mit richtig ✓ oder falsch - !**

1. There were a lot of spaces in the church at the funeral. ❐
2. Everyone blames the band for the murder. ❐
3. Andy spoke at the funeral. ❐
4. Sam doesn't trust Susan. ❐
5. Sam thinks Susan wants to take over from Esther. ❐
6. Rick was Paul Tyne's best friend. ❐
7. Paul's family knew about the engagement. ❐
8. After the funeral, the band members went home. ❐

Probably due to a general **boredom** with the current financial crisis, nearly every national newspaper had a small piece on Paul Tyne; some were even on the front page. Esther bought four different newspapers from the newspaper shop: The Times, The Independent,

The Daily Mail and The Sun. She made her way slowly back to her room and spread the newspapers on the bed.

The pictures of Paul broke another dam in Esther's mind. Although her feelings were still frozen to a large extent, she suddenly realized that she had loved Paul. Sadness filled her, but it was the kind of sadness that doesn't really touch you, like watching a report on the news about a natural disaster in a faraway country. It was a detached sort of grief.

Strange as it was, Esther felt more for Mrs Tarbitt's third son, Joshua, whom she had only known for two days. The six-year-old had taken quite a shine to Esther and used every excuse he could to come and sit with her. To begin with, Esther had sent him away, but his persistence was touching. By Monday, she was glad of the company, so he was soon coming and going as he pleased. Mrs Tarbitt knocked once or twice to find out if Joshua was bothering Esther – otherwise the two of them were left on their own at the top of the house. It was their oasis of calm above the continuous pandemonium caused by Joshua's siblings on the floors below.

The visits helped to distract Esther. She was happy that Susan had answered her mail so quickly, but at the same time, she was unsure whether sending it had been such a good idea after all. Could she trust Susan? On the one hand, she had hoped for an answer, and on the other, she had not expected it. It was now Tuesday midday. She took the £10 phone card out of her pocket for the hundredth time and put it down on the table.

to glare at sb.	jdn. anstarren
to get on with sb.	sich mit jdm. gut verstehen
delighted	begeistert, erfreut
boredom	Langeweile
grief	Trauer
↯ to take a shine to sb.	einen Narren an jdm. fressen
persistence	Hartnäckigkeit
pandemonium	Tumult
siblings *pl*	Geschwister
to distract	ablenken

Could it be a mistake to call her? She sighed. How many times had she already asked herself that question?
Accommodation, food and some new pieces of clothing had severely reduced the £300 that she had "borrowed" from Mrs Watson. Soon she would either have to "borrow" some more money or find a friend to help her, she realized. It was time to make a decision. She picked up the card and the door key, and the piece of paper with Susan's number.

Detective Inspector Mulligan was beginning to find the Radcliffe case intriguing. Forensics had confirmed that the drugs found on the floor of the hotel room were not the same as the drugs found in the suspect's blood. Esther Radcliffe's blood had revealed a dangerous cocktail of "date rape drugs", including Rohypnol and GHB, which produced nasty side effects like hallucination and amnesia. In fact, Peter Ford, head of the forensics department, had expressed his opinion on the matter very clearly.
"It's a miracle that she is here at all. She must have the **constitution** of an ox and the heart of a lion."
"If she's so strong, then do you think she could have killed her manager after all?" the DI asked.
Peter Ford gave a dry laugh. "Not if she had already taken those drugs."
Detective Sergeant Dawson leaned forward. "Could somebody have fed her the drugs during the evening? The other band members said that she appeared to be drunk fairly early on, which is why they left her there on her own."
"If that were the case, then she would have been unable to pick herself up, let alone the lamp," Ford replied.
"But then why would she have run away?" Mulligan wondered. "If what you say is true, she wouldn't even have known about the murder."

constitution	Verfassung
at all events	auf alle Fälle
to assume	annehmen
to sneeze	niesen

"Perhaps somebody at the hospital told her," said Dawson.
"At all events, she must have been very confused when she woke up," Ford added. "Most people who have been given such drugs suffer temporary, sometimes even permanent amnesia. It is very unlikely that she can remember much about the evening. She will be emotionally unstable and pretty unpredictable."
"So you're saying that she is potentially dangerous?" Mulligan said.
Ford pushed his heavy black glasses back on his nose. "It all depends on her nature, of course. Such drugs affect the emotions. Some people become very aggressive, others totally detached, almost autistic. Both can be very dangerous in the wrong person."
Mulligan stood up and started pacing up and down his office.
Thinking out loud he said, "Basically, then, we can assume that the poor woman has been framed and is now running for her life with no idea how she got herself into the mess in the first place."
Ford shrugged his shoulders. "So it would seem," he agreed.
Dawson groaned loudly, "Oh hell, Rawlins."
Ford frowned, "What's the matter?"
Mulligan grunted. "Our 'star' student PC Rawlins probably very kindly told the murderer or murderers where to find Esther Radcliffe. Now they are probably looking for her, too – to finish off the job."
He turned to Dawson, "I want men watching every member of the band. I don't even want them to sneeze without my knowing about it. We need to get down to Plymouth immediately."

When Susan's mobile phone rang at lunchtime, she was sitting on her sofa reading the newspaper. She jumped. She felt pretty sure she knew who it would be. She let it ring while she lit a cigarette. It trembled between her fingers as she picked up the phone.

Exercise 33: Unscramble the paragraph. **Lesen Sie weiter und korrigieren Sie die Reihenfolge des folgenden Gespräches!**

a) "Oh, Esther, I'm so relieved you've called. I've been so worried. Where are you? How are you?"

b) "I'm better than I was. When I first woke up, I couldn't even remember my name. Now my memory is gradually coming back, but I still need a bit of time before I go to the police."

c) Esther chose to answer the second question first. She wondered if anybody was sitting near Susan and listening to the conversation.

d) "Hello, Susan. It's me."

e) "Hello?"

1	2	3	4

"Of course you do," agreed Susan vehemently. "I can help you. What do you need? Clothes, money? Where can we meet?"

"Do you know if the police are watching you?"

Susan laughed. "No, they only have eyes for you..!"

The line went silent for a minute.

"Esther, are you still there?"

"Yes."

"What's the matter?"

"What happened, Susan? I can't remember much about the evening."

Susan breathed in deeply. She would have to **play her cards right** or Esther would never trust her.

"So you can't remember anything about the murder?"
"Not much. I remember that there was another man in the room with me – and perhaps another person, too?"
"Oh good. Then you may soon be able to remember who it was."
"Yes, I suppose so." Esther did not sound **convinced**.
"We should meet. It is important. I can tell you more about what happened, but I want to be sitting opposite you when I tell you."
"Can you get down to Plymouth?"
"Is that where you are?" Susan asked.
"When could you be there?"
"I could get down there this evening."
"Take your phone with you. I will call you again at around 6:00 p.m."
The line went dead.
"Esther…? Are you still there?"
Silence.

to play one's cards right	seine Trümpfe richtig ausspielen
convinced	überzeugt

Exercise 34: Remind and remember. Wählen Sie die richtige Alternative!

1. He reminded / remembered me of my grandfather.
2. Could you remember / remind me of his name?
3. How do you remember / remind all those facts?
4. I will only remind / remember you once, Rick!
5. Jean reminded / remembered that she had an appointment.

Susan put the phone down and closed her eyes for a moment. When she opened them again, something cold and yet dark flashed within them. "Yes, do let me remind you of that horrible evening, my *friend*," she murmured.

Jean, Bill and Rick were already halfway to Plymouth by the time Susan packed the minivan. They had left at about the same time – Jean and Bill in one car, Rick in another – perfectly unaware of the fact that they were travelling in the same direction.

Neither Jean and Bill nor Rick had a plan. Rick simply hoped that Esther would phone him as instructed by Susan, while Jean and Bill had booked themselves a room in Plymouth and meant to drive round the streets looking for her – the proverbial needle in the haystack.

proverbial	sprichwörtlich
sense	*hier*: Vernunft
in conversational mood	gesprächig
moodily	launisch

Bill was not optimistic about their chances of success.

"If she has any sense, she will probably have moved on by now," he grumbled.

Jean was more optimistic. "Esther is an expert at changing her appearance, thanks to me, so she's going to feel pretty safe once she's found a place to stay."

"Hopefully, we'll get to her before the others do," Bill said grimly.

Precisely the same thought was going through the minds of Susan, Rick, Mulligan and Dawson – all of whom were somewhere on the M4 and M5 motorways heading towards Plymouth.

It was a beautiful summer afternoon and Detective Sergeant Dawson was looking forward to continuing the investigation in Devon. He was in conversational mood. Mulligan, on the other hand, was staring moodily at the traffic on the motorway, occasionally swearing angrily when lorries pulled out into the middle lane in front of him.

Exercise 35: Simple past or present perfect. Lesen Sie weiter und setzen Sie die Verben in die richtige Zeitform!

"I **1.** phone ________________ the Woods International Resort this morning and booked us in there, as you suggested," Dawson said.

"I know. You told me."

" **2.** speak ________________ to Mrs Watson yet?"

"No."

" **3.** get ________________ any more news from the station in Plymouth?"

"No."

"So we still **4.** receive ________________ anything to indicate that she is on the move."

"No."

And that **5.** be ________________ all Dawson could get out of Mulligan.

Dawson knew Mulligan. He did not want to speak because he was already working on their investigation in Plymouth. His boss was physically with him in the car, but mentally he was searching for

Esther Radcliffe. The dark eyebrows had joined together in a long line, and there was that hard, determined expression on the detective's face. Dawson leant back to watch the English countryside **whizzing past**. He knew better than to **press his luck** by pushing Mulligan to "chat" when he was working.

to whiz past	vorbeisausen
to press one's luck	sein Schicksal herausfordern
to turn out to be	sich entpuppen als
to relish	genießen, Gefallen finden an

Esther didn't call until 6:15 p.m. She had not been able to find a public telephone that was working. When she did, she had to wait ten minutes for an Italian student to finish his weekly call to mama.

Susan answered the phone immediately. Esther felt waves of relief running through her body. She was no longer totally alone.

"Hello Susan. Where are you?"

"I'm in Plymouth. Where shall we meet?"

"At the Royal Victoria Inn Restaurant," Esther suggested.

"Where's that?"

"On the road towards Saltash on the Plymouth side of the estuary.[i] The restaurant is always crowded with railway enthusiasts, so nobody will take much notice of us if we meet in the car park there. I am already here, so you can come when you are ready."

"I'll come straight away," Susan replied.

Die Mündung des Flusses Tamar liegt westlich von Plymouth. Plymouth und Saltash verbindet die Tamar Bridge, die bei ihrer Eröffnung im Jahre 1961 die längste Hängebrücke Englands war.

At 6:00 p.m. in Saltash, Detective Inspector Mulligan, Detective Sergeant Dawson and Mary Watson were sitting out on the terrace of the Woods International Resort. The two detectives had ordered themselves a coffee and a glass of Pinot Grigio for Mary Watson.

The cheerful pensioner, who turned out to be a surprisingly good golfer, had been more than happy to talk about the events of the past Thursday evening. In fact, she seemed to relish being the centre of attention. Like the fisherman talking about his catch, the story had become bigger and bigger the more often she had told it. Luckily, Mulligan had the police report and was able to ignore some of the more flowery details. What he really wanted to know was what Esther Radcliffe had taken from Mary Watson's suitcase.

Exercise 36: Questions. **Fragen Sie nach den markierten Satzteilen!**

1. Detective Inspector Mulligan was thinking **about the case.**

____

2. The murder took place **on Wednesday.**

____

3. Susan and Esther are going to meet **at the Royal Victoria Inn Restaurant.**

____

4. Esther called **Susan.**

____

5. Nobody will notice them **because the restaurant is full.**

____

"Mrs Watson, could you please describe the clothing and other articles which Esther Radcliffe stole from your suitcase."
"She took two open-necked t-shirts, one blue and one red, a green anorak, some tennis socks, one of my favourite Hermes scarves and my bedside torch."
Mary Watson had been asked this question a few times, Mulligan realized.
"And of course," she continued, "the three hundred pounds she found hidden in the zipped compartment at the bottom, as well as some things from the bathroom."
"Three hundred pounds?" Mulligan read the notes he had received from the Plymouth constabulary.
"This report doesn't mention the three hundred pounds."
The old lady frowned. "Well, I definitely told the young man about it."
"Ah, never mind," Mulligan smiled as he made a mental note to shout at another PC. "It just goes to show that two heads are better than one!"

It just goes to show...	Da sieht man mal wieder ...
to beam	strahlen
hedge	Hecke
frumpy	altbacken

Mulligan and Dawson stood up. Mrs Watson seemed surprised and slightly disappointed that the interview was already over.
"That's actually all I need to know," Mulligan said, giving the old lady a big smile. He leant forward to shake her hand. "Thank you so much for your time, Mrs Watson. If only everybody were like you."
"Why thank you," beamed Mrs Watson.

Esther had found a table outside with a good view of the car park entrance, so she immediately saw Susan when she drove up in a shiny black minivan. Esther felt fairly exposed sitting outside and was glad when she saw Susan slowly drive to the far end of the car park and pull into a space by some trees and a tall hedge.

Clever, Esther thought. Nobody will see us there. She called the waiter over and paid for her drink, and then waited until she saw Susan walking towards the restaurant. Susan was wearing an elegant blue linen trouser suit and high heels, which made her walk like a model on the catwalk. She was dressed more for tea with the queen than a pub meal. Her bright red lipstick and low-cut top also did nothing to help her merge into the background.

Exercise 37: Translation quiz. Übersetzen Sie und enträtseln Sie das Lösungswort!

1. Kleidung _ _ _ _ _ _ _ □
2. enttäuschen _ _ _ _ _ _ □ _ _ _
3. blumig _ □ _ _ _ _ _
4. Stirnrunzeln □ _ _ _ _
5. fröhlich _ _ _ □ _ _ _ _
6. Bericht □ _ _ _ _ _

Lösung: _ _ _ _ _ _

Esther frowned slightly as she noticed how all male heads automatically turned in Susan's direction, but then she smiled and felt almost relaxed. At least nobody would bother with the attractive woman's frumpy friend. Perhaps Susan had dressed that way on purpose, in order to distract people.
Susan did not recognize Esther as she came down the steps from the restaurant. She would have walked straight past her if Esther hadn't touched her arm and said, "Hi Susan. It's great to see you!"

Susan stopped dead in her tracks. Her mouth opened and closed like a goldfish for a couple of seconds. Then she composed herself "I'm not sure I think much of the new outfit, Esther."

Exercise 38: Correct the mistakes. Lesen Sie weiter und korrigieren Sie die fünf Fehler im folgenden Absatz!

About ten miles away from Susan and Esther, DI Mulligan's handy rang.
"What do you mean, you only no where Sam Silver is?! I have asked you to keep an eye on all of them. They can't have disapeared into thin air. Get their registrar numbers and search for the cars IMMEDIATELY!"

1. ______________________________

2. ______________________________

3. ______________________________

4. ______________________________

5. ______________________________

Susan gave Esther a quick peck on the cheek.
"I'm pretty certain that nobody followed me, but I'm not one hundred per cent sure, so we'd better get moving," she whispered nervously. Esther nodded. There was something about Susan's behaviour that was making her even more frightened than she already was. Perhaps it had not been such a good idea to call her after all.

"You don't have to help me, you know. If you could just lend me a bit of money, that would be enough. You can drive straight back to London if you prefer. You don't need to get involved in this mess."
This seemed to panic Susan even more.
"No, Esther. I can't leave you like this. Forgive me. I'll calm down in a minute."
They started walking back across the car park, which was completely empty except for them.
"I hired the minivan in London," Susan added quickly, "in case the police thought to follow my car."
"A bit of a handful after the mini, I should think," Esther smiled, trying to make Susan relax a bit.
"You remember the mini then," said Susan, visibly trembling now.
Esther stopped again. "Yes, I can remember quite a few things now."
"You can…? That's great," Susan stuttered unconvincingly.
Esther suddenly felt very wary of her "friend". Why was she acting so strangely?
"Look, let's please just get in the car…"
Susan grasped Esther's arm. Her grip was clammy and cold. "Come on, we can sit in the back of the minivan for a while and just talk."
Some inner instinct told Esther to run. She turned back towards the restaurant, but it was too late. She did not even hear the man come out from behind the hedge with the ether-soaked rag. He pulled her round so that she was facing away from the restaurant and then forced the rag over her mouth. The last thing Esther saw before she passed out was Susan opening the back of the minivan.

to stop dead in one's tracks	wie angewurzelt stehenbleiben
to compose oneself	sich beruhigen, sich fassen
↯ peck	Küsschen
↯ a bit of a handful	*hier*: etw. schwierig
to grasp	etw. (fest) fassen
clammy	feuchtkalt
ether-soaked	in Äther getränkt
rag	Lumpen
to pass out	bewusstlos werden

Exercise 39: Antonyms. Finden Sie die Gegensatzpaare!

1.	☐ shouted	a) lend
2.	☐ freeze	b) accidentally
3.	☐ borrow	c) melt
4.	☐ on purpose	d) confident
5.	☐ nervous	e) whispered

6 IN TERROR

Esther woke up in her nightmare. She was lying on a mattress in a pitch black room. Fear filled her with the same cold darkness that surrounded her. Her forehead was bleeding slightly and she was trembling uncontrollably. Moonlight shone weakly through a tiny barred window, and the sound of an owl on a tree nearby made her cry out in alarm.

For a while, she did not move, scared at what she would discover around her. Then, in panic, she started crawling about blindly, her arms outstretched, looking for a way out. The mattress was on a dirty concrete floor in a small cell-like room. The "cell", an old bathroom, was about two by four metres and had brick walls and a thick wooden door without a handle on the inside.

pitch black	pechschwarz
to crawl	kriechen
hollow	Mulde, Vertiefung
weeds *pl*	Unkraut
suffocating	stickig
musty	muffig
damp	feucht

Apart from the mattress, there was only an old toilet and a tiny basin in one corner. The room was half below ground level and there was a hollow outside the window which was full of weeds. There was a suffocating, musty smell of damp and dust.

Esther moved back to the mattress and lay down. She tried to control her fear by focusing her mind on what had happened. She was totally confused. Why would Susan lock her up in a cellar? Was she

the person who had pushed her back onto the sofa on the night of the murder? Did she have something to do with the crime?
In the darkness, Esther heard Paul's last cry again: "I love you, Esther. I will always love you."
Pictures of the two of them together filled Esther's head, and at last the deep love that she, too, had felt for Paul flooded up to the surface of her consciousness. They had been very happy together. She knew that now. They had wanted to announce their engagement and at last to end the secrecy.
As Esther sat alone in the dark cell, it was not fear that made her cry, but grief. Tears started to run down her face, and soon she was sobbing uncontrollably. Only one good thing came out of that terrible night as she fell in and out of sleep: she could never have killed Paul. She had loved him more than she had loved herself.

Exercise 40: Word order. Lesen Sie weiter und korrigieren Sie die Wortstellung im folgenden Absatz!

Detective Inspector Mulligan was still awake also. However, Esther unlike, he was sitting on a hotel comfortable bed and watching a night-late film. He and Peter Dawson had a nice meal eaten in the restaurant hotel. They then arranged to meet when the following morning before to their respective rooms going. Next to him, had Mulligan a notebook and from the minibar a glass of whisky.

After talking to Mrs Watson, he and Peter had gone down to the station in Plymouth to speak to PC Duncan, but had learned nothing really new from the young policeman. The constable had simply confirmed that Mrs Watson had told him about the three hundred pounds. Mulligan's faith in the new generation **dwindled** further, but he kept his comments to himself.

His initial plan had been to stay at the Woods International Resort, but the rooms were expensive, so he and Dawson found a cheap hotel in Carkeel just outside Saltash.

"She probably **slept rough** the first night, so no wonder nobody saw her," Peter had remarked as they passed through miles of beautiful Cornish countryside.

"I can think of worse places to do that," Mulligan agreed **grumpily**.

to sob	schluchzen
respective	jeweilig, entsprechend
to dwindle	schwinden
to sleep rough	im Freien übernachten
grumpily	mürrisch

"Don't you think it would be better if you went home, sir?" asked the barman politely when Rick ordered a sixth glass of gin and tonic. Rick glared at the young man from behind his dark sunglasses. The barman wasn't much older than Rick, but he was beginning to sound like his father.
"I'll de-shide when I'm go-wing home, not you," he slurred. "Anyway, I'm a guesht here, so you can carry me up to my room if necess-ss-ary." The barman shrugged his shoulders and mixed another gin and tonic. Richard sat there for a while longer, drumming on his glass with a couple of toothpicks, then he threw a ten-pound note on the bar. "Keep the shange. I'm taking thish one up-shares."

Exercise 41: Odd one out. Welches Wort ist das „schwarze Schaf"? Unterstreichen Sie!

1. damp wet clammy dry
2. notice observe recognize ignore
3. increase decline dwindle reduce
4. statement story account report

He managed to get to his room without spilling the drink completely and put it down on the small table next to the window. His plan to drown his sorrows hadn't really worked. He decided to return to London first thing the following day. Esther had had her chance.

Just a few streets away in the Astoria Hotel, Jean and Bill were drinking a nightcap in the lounge. Bill had pretended to be Mulligan to get some information out of a young, inexperienced PC at the Plymouth police station. He had told them that Esther had been at the

Woods International Resort and that she was still probably in the area. It was not much, yet it was enough to make them feel that they should stay a bit longer.

"We must find her. I **owe** it to Paul," Jean **sniffed**, pulling a handkerchief out of her bag. "He was always so good to me."

Bill patted her hand. "Come on, luv. This isn't like you to be emotional. We'll find her."

Jean managed a smile and stood up. "Yes, yes, of course, you're right. I don't know what came over me. I'm going to bed before I make a complete idiot of myself. Shall we meet at 8:00 a.m. for breakfast?"

"That's fine with me," replied Bill, standing up to say goodnight. When she had gone, he sat down and drank the rest of his brandy. He was not as optimistic as he had tried to make her believe. Finding Esther really was going to be hard.

to slur	lallen
to spill	verschütten
to drown one's sorrows	seine Sorgen in Alkohol ertränken
nightcap	Schlummertrunk, Absacker
to owe sb. sth.	jdm. etw. schuldig sein
to sniff	*hier*: schniefen

Exercise 42: Pronouns. Lesen Sie weiter und setzen Sie die fehlenden Pronomen ein!

Susan's shouting woke Esther from her restless sleep the following morning.

" **1.** ______ said that you were going to take **2.** ______ to the police station, Sam! That's the only reason why **3.** ______ helped you."

There was the sound of a face being **slapped**. Esther sat up quickly.

"I know that **4.** ______ and Paul were almost like brothers, but you can't take the law into **5.** ______ own hands."

Susan was crying now. "It won't bring **6.** ______ back. What are you going to do with that knife? Give **7.** ______ to me! Please, Sam, don't do anything silly!"

A door slammed.

"Susan, you've got to help me," Esther screamed. "I didn't kill Paul, I promise you!"

Silence. Absolute silence.

While DS Dawson was **tucking into** a full English breakfast[i] of bacon, egg, sausage and fried bread, DI Mulligan announced that he intended to **step up** the search for Esther.

"I want her photograph in the local papers, and as many constables as possible going from door to door with her picture."

"Why the sudden change of mind?" Dawson asked.

Das **Full English Breakfast** besteht aus drei Gängen: Auf Fruchtsaft und Müsli bzw. Porridge folgt ein warmer Hauptgang u. a. mit Speck, Ei und gebackenen Bohnen. Den Abschluss bildet Toast mit gesalzener Butter und Orangenmarmelade.

"I don't want the murderers catching up with her first," Mulligan said, sipping his coffee.

Dawson took out his phone and walked out onto the hotel terrace to make a phone call and smoke a cigarette. When he came back, he seemed **concerned**.

"What's the matter? Did they make any difficulties?"

"No, but PC Duncan thought you would perhaps like to know that when we were talking to Mary Watson at the Woods International Resort, another Detective Inspector Mulligan phoned and received a detailed report of the case from one of the trainees."

to slap	eine Ohrfeige geben
ϟ to tuck into	(mit Appetit) essen
to step up	verstärken
concerned	besorgt
expletives	Schimpfwörter
impenetrable	unüberwindlich
to mull over	sich durch den Kopf gehen lassen
inconceivable	undenkbar

Mulligan's stream of **expletives** quite shocked an old couple enjoying their bacon and egg at the next table.

In the meantime, Esther was pretty sure that she was completely alone in the house. She had shouted for help through the window for a while, but had soon given up. It was clear that nobody could hear her. The silence outside the small window, except for birdsong, told her that she was probably right out in the middle of the countryside. She drank some water from the tap and tried to ignore her grumbling stomach. She had not eaten properly since breakfast the previous day – and that seemed like a lifetime ago.

The only possible escape from the room was through the door, but without the key or at least an axe, it was **impenetrable**. She was just going to have to wait and hope that somebody found her.

She **mulled over** what she had heard outside the door. It seemed so **inconceivable** to her that Sam could have anything to do with the murder. Yes, he had been Paul's closest friend, but Sam had been a close friend of hers, too. Over the years, the three of them had been through thick and thin together. Sam was going to be their **best man**. He had known their secret.

The loss of his best friend would have hit him hard. He and Paul had played football in the same school team, had gone fishing together and even, occasionally, fallen in love with the same girl. He would be in total shock at the moment – but murder …?

Esther shook her head. Despite her general uncertainty about what exactly had happened, that just did not make sense. Sam **despised** Susan. Why would he ask her for help? And if they had gone to the trouble to kidnap her, then why not question her? It seemed so illogical. Esther shook her head again. Something did not quite add up. She started pacing up and down. Paul would want her to fight. She was not going to **give in** yet.

best man	Trauzeuge
to despise	verachten
to give in	aufgeben
to presume	davon ausgehen

Down at Plymouth Police Station, DI Mulligan was "gently" reminding his colleagues about security regulations when providing information over the phone, when his own phone rang. It was PC Rawlins.

"I hope that you have some good news for me, Rawlins," he growled.

"Yes, sir, I think so," Rawlins replied. "We have managed to locate three of the missing band members: Andrew Button, Susan Ellington and Richard Marks. They were all seen walking into the Piccadilly studio this morning, with Sam Silver."

"What about Jean Jary and Bill Perez?"

"Well, sir, I spoke to Jean Jary's daughter. She told me that her mother had phoned her from some hotel, although she wouldn't tell her where she was. Her daughter was a bit worried and wrote

down the telephone number on her display. I've just phoned the number. It's the Astoria Hotel in Plymouth."
"Are they staying there?"

Exercise 43: Phrasal verbs. Setzen Sie die richtigen Präpositionen ein!

about | in | over | out | up

1. Esther was determined. She did not want to give ___.
2. She sat down and mulled ___ what she had heard.
3. Dawson looked ___ the address in the telephone book.
4. If he drinks any more he is going to pass ___.
5. Mulligan was concerned ___ Esther.

"Yes, sir! They haven't checked out yet. Apparently they're out at the moment, looking at different golf courses. Another interesting thing was that the man on the front desk told me that Mr Perez had asked him for the telephone number of the Plymouth police station the day before."
"Our other Mulligan, I presume...," muttered the detective.
"Sir?" Rawlins asked.

"Okay, Rawlins. Sergeant Dawson and I will find Jean Jary and Bill Perez. You just make sure that none of the other band members disappear again."
"Yes, sir."
"And Rawlins…"
"Yes, sir?"
"Good work, keep it up."
DS Dawson looked up from the computer, somewhat surprised by Mulligan's rare words of praise.
"Good news?" he asked.
"Not sure. I'll tell you about it in the car. We need to get over to the Woods International Resort asap. We might be lucky and find the 'other Mulligan' chatting to Mrs Watson. Doesn't she have her golf lessons in the morning?"
"Yes, until 1:00 p.m. as far as I remember."
"And it's just gone one, so let's all get over there pronto!"

praise	Lob
asap (= as soon as possible)	schnellstmöglich

Mrs Watson was a bit surprised when yet another detective turned up to interview her, but she enjoyed the attention too much to be suspicious. She was just telling the detective and his female assistant about the three hundred pounds when Mulligan and Dawson stormed into the lobby, followed by two uniformed police officers.
The furious look on DI Mulligan's face made even the cheerful Mrs Watson nervous.
"My goodness!" she exclaimed. "Four detectives from Scotland Yard and two police officers. I do[i] feel important."
Bill Perez made a move to stand up, but DS Dawson put a hand on his shoulder.
"Please stay where you are, Mr Perez."
"I can explain…," Bill Perez began.

In unverneinten Aussagesätzen verleiht ein hinzugefügtes **do** dem folgenden Verb im Infinitiv besonderen Nachdruck.

Exercise 44: Crossword puzzle. Lösen Sie das Kreuzworträtsel!

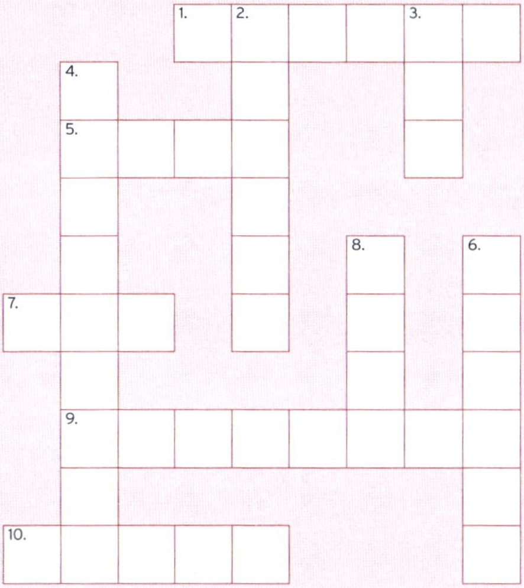

Across

1. Esther sees no way to ... from the cell.
5. Jean Jary's daughter has no ... where her mother is.
7. An old piece of cloth used e.g. for cleaning.
9. A person who is in a prison is a ...
10. He tried to ... his sorrows in a bottle of whisky.

Down

2. During the tourist ..., the streets of Saltash are filled with people.
3. You sit on this at church.
4. A person who holds someone against their will.
6. Police organized a ... for the missing child.
8. The source of light outside Esther's window at night.

"You will have ample time for that, Mr Perez," Mulligan snapped. "I am arresting you and Ms Jary for impersonating police officers." He glanced over to the two police officers behind him. "Please take these two down to the station and put them in the cells. I'll be along shortly."
After they had all left, Mulligan's expression relaxed.
"I am so sorry, Mrs Watson. You're not having much luck at the moment with the people you meet, are you?"
Surprisingly, Mary Watson did not seem the least upset. "My husband, bless his soul, always said I was gullible. He's probably laughing at me right now. Perhaps I'll learn something from the experience, you never know?"
Even Mulligan had to smile at the widow's reaction. "It's never too late to learn, Mrs Watson."

Exercise 45: Synonyms. Welche Wörter gehören zusammen? Ordnen Sie zu!

1. ☐	worried	a) naive
2. ☐	inconceivable	b) furious
3. ☐	presume	c) concerned
4. ☐	gullible	d) assume
5. ☐	very angry	e) unthinkable

It was the first time that the Ballads and Balladies (or rather Ballady) had ever met to see what the songs would sound like with Susan instead of Esther singing. They tried out some of the easier

ballads just to get warmed up, and then moved on to the songs planned for the next concerts.
Susan was in her element. She sang powerfully, she looked good and was a sexy dancer. That was what made her such an excellent backing vocalist. However, Susan had always believed that she **had what it took** to be a lead singer. It had never been necessary to disillusion her. Unfortunately, during the course of the afternoon, it became increasingly clear that the time had come.
Sam hoped that either Rick or Andy would eventually say something. When, after three hours, Susan began killing one of his favourite songs, Sam **reached the end of his tether**. He slammed his hands down on the keys with such force that everyone else stopped what they were doing.
"This is absolutely ridiculous," he **fumed**. "Andy, for heaven's sake! Aren't you going to say anything? You always had enough to say when Esther was singing."
Andy's face took on a stubborn look. "I think Susan **deserves** a chance. She has a good voice. Of course, she's not going to have Esther's quality straight away."
Now it was Susan's turn to glare at Sam and then Andy. "What are you two talking about? I think this **rehearsal** is going really well. People will love my voice. It's stronger than Esther's. They're ready for a change."
"Not this sort of change, they're not," said Rick quietly. "If you go to a gig and sing the way you have this afternoon, they are going to laugh us right off the stage."

ample	reichlich, genügend
gullible	leichtgläubig
widow	Witwe
⚡ to have what it takes	das Zeug zu etw. haben
to reach the end of one's tether	mit der Geduld am Ende sein
to fume	vor Wut toben
to deserve	verdienen (Leistung)
rehearsal	Probe

Susan's face hardened and her lips tightened into a straight line. "Look, I'm all you've got – if you want Ballads and Balladies to survive, that is."
With that, Susan turned on her heel and left the room.
After the door closed behind her, Rick rested his sticks on a drum and took out a packet of cigarettes. "So, where do we go from here?"
"The job centre by the looks of things," Sam retorted moodily.

Exercise 46: Conjunctions. **Lesen Sie weiter und setzen Sie die folgenden Konjunktionen richtig ein!**

as soon as | when | if | because | as | until | whether | while

1. ______ Mulligan got back to the station, he sat down with Dawson to finish putting together the information for the local newspapers. 2. ______ he was on the phone to a colleague at Scotland Yard, PC Duncan came in. 3. ______ he put the phone down, he asked 4. ______ he should bring Jean Jary and Bill Perez up from the cells 5. ______ it was getting late. Mulligan shook his head.
"No, let them wait 6. ______ we have finished here," Mulligan replied.

He knew that they were sitting nervously in the cells downstairs. Experience had taught him that **7.** ______ he left suspects in the cell for a bit longer, they tended to be more cooperative **8.** ______ they were so nervous.

Mulligan was right again. By the time Jean Jary and Bill Perez were brought up from the cells, they were each as meek as a lamb.
"So you admit that you phoned this station and pretended to be me phoning about the case," Mulligan questioned Perez.
"Yes, Inspector, I did impersonate you."
"And why?"
"We are very worried about Esther, Inspector. I know that you and your team are investigating the case, but you think that Esther committed the crime. Jean and I don't think that, and we're also afraid that somebody may be following her."

meek as a lamb	lammfromm
down-to-earth	bodenständig
record	*hier*: Akte
to blush	erröten

Although Mulligan was not sure if he could trust Jean Jary, there was something down-to-earth about Bill Perez. He had read the ex-policeman's record earlier and found out that Perez had been an excellent policeman. That was until a gunshot wound had ended the officer's career.
Mulligan turned his attention to Jean Jary, who was a pale shadow of her former confident self.
"Ms Jary, you told me at our last meeting that on the night of the murder you heard other voices in the hotel room. Why didn't you go in?"
Bill Perez cleared his throat very loudly and frowned.
Jean Jary blushed and looked down.

"I'm sorry, Inspector, but that was a lie. I was nowhere near the room when the murder occurred, so I didn't hear anything."
Mulligan sighed. He made a couple of notes, stood up and walked over to the window. Without bothering to look round he growled, "You can both go, although I should really keep you in custody for obstructing police business with your lies! I expect you to return to London immediately and to report to me at Scotland Yard tomorrow."

Exercise 47: Active voice. Setzen Sie die passiven Sätze ins Aktiv!

1. The road was blocked by the police.

   ____

2. Esther was pulled into the minivan by the kidnappers.

   ____

3. The witnesses were told by the police to stay in town.

   ____

4. The murderer was arrested yesterday.

   ____

5. The accused was found guilty by the jury.

   ____

6. The victim was hit with a lamp by the murderer.

   ____

Dark clouds had taken away the little bit of light left in the cellar, and all of Esther's fears returned. She sat trembling with cold and hunger in the darkness. It had been raining heavily, and the hollow outside the window was filling up with water. Slowly at first and then more quickly, the water started to seep and then stream in through the window. With it came two rats and a lot of dirt. Esther moved into the corner next to the door with the mattress. Some of the water escaped under the door, but the gap underneath was far too narrow for the rats. Esther could hear the rodents that she could not see – occasionally she could feel them, too…

custody	Gewahrsam
to obstruct	behindern
to seep	sickern
rodent	Nagetier

7 MOTIVE MAZE

Mrs Tarbitt was getting a bit worried about her tenant. She had not returned to the room in over twenty-four hours. Joshua was beside himself.

"Mummy, we must go to the police. Somebody might have hurt her. She wouldn't go away without telling us."

Mrs Tarbitt was not so sure about that because she had rented the room to enough shady characters in the past to recognize a person with a secret. On the other hand, Cynthia Banks, or whoever she was, had paid her rent until the end of the week. Mrs Tarbitt looked into her son's tear-filled eyes.

"Look, darling, I'll tell you what. If she doesn't come home tomorrow, we'll go to the police, I promise."

Although she was not normally one to pry, she decided to go into the room to try and find out if her tenant had left for good.

When she walked into the room, she was surprised at how tidy it was. Everything was put away; the bed was made and, apart from a coffee cup on the draining board, there was nothing to show that someone was living there. Out of curiosity, Mrs Tarbitt peeked into the wardrobe. Cynthia Banks travelled very light. There were some t-shirts in the

maze	Labyrinth
↯ shady	zwielichtig
to pry	herumschnüffeln
draining board	Abtropfbrett
sachet	Beutel
landlady	Zimmerwirtin, Vermieterin

wardrobe, a red beret and some sunglasses and a couple of cheap summer dresses. Otherwise, there were just some old newspapers, a small rucksack and one pair of flat shoes.
Mrs Tarbitt closed the door quickly, feeling slightly embarrassed. She walked into the bathroom next. There was a luxurious white towel with some sort of emblem on it and some toiletries, including a toothbrush. In the bin was an empty sachet. Mrs Tarbitt recognized it and smiled. Obviously, auburn was not Ms Banks' natural hair colour.
A final look, this time into the fridge, which was absolutely full, told the landlady that Cynthia's absence was not intended to be long term. Perhaps something really had happened to her guest and she should go straight to the police. On the other hand, if Cynthia Banks wanted to stay incognito, Mrs Tarbitt wouldn't be doing her any favours by going to the police. She decided to wait until the following evening. If the woman had not returned by then, she would take steps. She looked out of the window at the pouring rain. Hopefully her tenant had a jacket with her.
"Mummmyyy," shouted Lizzie up the stairs. "Joshua has put honey on my homework."
Mrs Tarbitt sighed and headed down the stairs. By the time she was in the kitchen, Cynthia Banks was no longer a concern.

Exercise 48: Choose the correct alternative. Lesen Sie weiter und unterstreichen Sie die richtige Variante!

It was **1.** an / a extremely long night for Esther. The rain was constant and unending. **2.** Each / Every five minutes or so, another wave of water and dirt poured through the small window into the cellar. Esther spent **3.** the most of / most of the night **perched** on the sink with her feet on the toilet, using the thin mattress as a backrest. After a while, water started to fill her cell **4.** more quickly / quicklier. She pulled her knees up to her chest and stared at the water **with chattering teeth**. There **5.** had to be / should be a river nearby, Esther realized.

When the water reached the height of the sink, she jumped off it and waded to the window. She grabbed the bars and started screaming wildly for help.

About 180 miles away in a dry, comfortable bed, Sam Silver lay awake thinking. He was not screaming, but he was not happy either. This time a week ago, he and the band had woken up to discover that instead of being at the beginning of a big breakthrough, they were involved in a murder case. Now, in the space of a week, the band was falling apart. Without Esther, the band didn't work. Susan could not replace Esther and a new lead singer would mean the formation of a new band.

"Why, Esther?" he shouted at the ceiling. "It just makes no sense."

DI Mulligan was having the same problem as Sam. Unable to sleep, the detective got up and went into work at 6:00 a.m. He made himself a coffee and sat straight down to look at his mails.

PC Duncan had written to say that the Plymouth Herald was putting the story on the front page with a photograph and that posters

had been hung in all major public places within a 25-mile radius. In his pile of post, he also discovered an unsigned, anonymous postcard.
It read: "Ask Sam Silver where he was on the evening of the murder. Ask him about his relationship with Esther."
Mulligan sat examining the card carefully, and at precisely 7:00 a.m., he phoned Dawson. "I want to drop in on the other band members this morning and ask them a few more questions. I don't think Ms Jary is the only one who has been lying to us."

to perch	hocken (wie ein Vogel)
with chattering teeth	zähneklappernd
stench	Gestank
unbearable	unerträglich
to starve	verhungern
eve	Vorabend

Luckily, the water level did not rise above the sink. In the early hours of the morning, it sank almost as quickly as it had risen, although the stench of what remained was almost unbearable.
As it grew lighter, Esther saw that the floor was covered with leaves, rusty nails, empty tins and pieces of wood. Everything was cold and wet. Using a small piece of wood, she managed to push most of the rubbish into one corner. She then used water from the sink to slowly wash away as much of the dirt as possible, both on herself and on the floor. It kept her busy and distracted her from the growing fear that not even her kidnappers were coming back to get her and that she was going to starve to death in the deserted house.
As she knelt on the floor, dirty and so alone, the concert from the week before seemed so unreal. At the time, it felt as if she had been at the beginning of something big. She had felt like a star on the eve of a great career. Now, she was nothing more than a frightened animal – desperate and alone.

To fight away her terror, she forced herself to remember the concert in detail. Paul had stood nearby the whole time, watching her, and she had looked at him again and again as she sang.
"So look at me now," sighed Esther, as she **rinsed** her top for the second time.

Exercise 49: True or false? **Welche Aussagen sind korrekt? Markieren Sie mit richtig ✓ oder falsch – !**

1. Mrs Tarbitt wanted to report her tenant missing straight away. ❐
2. The water in Esther's cell reached her neck. ❐
3. Esther tried to clear away the dirt. ❐
4. Mulligan wanted to call the band back down to the station. ❐
5. Mulligan and Sam both could not sleep. ❐

"Where do you want to go first?" Dawson asked after he got into Mulligan's car.
"Sam Silver is the closest, then Richard Marks and, afterwards, Andrew Button and Susan Ellington."
It was not yet quite 8:00 a.m., but the traffic on the London roads was already quite busy. Everybody seemed to be in a rush. Children in school uniforms ran to catch double-decker buses, while moped couriers **weaved** dangerously between large cars with **immaculately** dressed businessmen. It was going to be a hot day.

They reached Sam Silver's road at 8:15 a.m. The pianist lived in a **loft residence** in Lambeth. He opened the door in his dressing gown.

"Good morning, Mr Silver," Mulligan said. "Can we come in?"

Sam paled, but opened the door to let them in. He led them into a **spacious** and very light room with high ceilings. It was dominated by a **grand piano**.

to rinse	auswaschen
to weave	*hier*: sich durchschlängeln
immaculately	makellos
loft residence	Loft
spacious	geräumig
grand piano	Flügel
fiancée	Verlobte

"We can sit down over there," said Sam, pointing to two leather sofas. "I've just made a coffee, do you want one?"

"No, we're fine," replied Mulligan, before Dawson had a chance to say "yes". "We only want to ask you a couple of questions."

Sam nodded nervously and picked up his own coffee before he sat down opposite them.

"Have you found Esther?" he asked.

"No," Mulligan answered. "We wanted to ask if, by chance, she had contacted you."

"No," Sam answered sadly. "I wish she had."

"How would you describe your relationship with Esther Radcliffe, Mr Silver?"

"Relationship? What do you mean?" Sam Silver seemed irritated by the question.

Achtung false friends

irritated	≠	irritiert
irritated		verärgert
confused		irritiert

"Were you friends? Did you see much of each other?"

"Of course we were friends," Sam snapped. "She was the **fiancée** of my best friend. And I saw her most days because, as you may remember, we worked together."

"Fiancée?" Mulligan questioned. "Was it official?"

"No," Sam replied. "For the press, we all thought it would be better if people thought that Andy and Esther were still together. But Esther left Andy for Paul months ago."

"And how did Andy feel about being **jilted**?"

Sam examined Mulligan's face, not sure about the implications of the question.

"Andy was upset of course, but then he and Susan got together, and since then I think he's been pretty cool about the whole thing."

Mulligan **scribbled** notes in his usual style: "AB jilted for PT, AB with SE, A initially annoyed?"

"Since then...?"

Sam was visibly uncomfortable with the question. "Look, Mr Mulligan, this is all subjective... Anybody who is jilted for someone else is going to be a bit upset about it."

Exercise 50: Unscramble. **Lesen Sie weiter und bringen Sie die Buchstaben in die richtige Reihenfolge!**

Mulligan smiled **1.** paneltyit ________________. "Yes, Mr Silver. But I am **2.** tingaivinestg ________________ a murder case, and every little **3.** ipeec of information about what people feel and think is important. Was Paul Tyne a **4.** arpulop ________________ man?"

Another short pause. Mulligan **5.** earlediz ________________ that Sam Silver was not a man to open his mouth without thinking.

"Paul, as I have already mentioned, was my best friend. He was a great friend and a great agent. But to be a good agent in the music business, you have to be pretty tough, both with yourself and others." Sam paused again. "That means that Paul was not always popular, even with the members of the band."
Another pause.
Mulligan leant forward. "Any special examples? What about Mr Marks?"
Sam frowned. "Rick enjoys the occasional illeg.."
He stopped, embarrassed.
"...illegal substance?" Mulligan finished the sentence for him.
"Erm... yes, but nothing really serious – a bit of pot and perhaps the occasional..., but I really don't know exactly," Sam stuttered.

to jilt	abservieren, den Laufpass geben
to scribble	kritzeln
ϟ pot	Marihuana
ϟ habit	Sucht
recording session	Aufnahmesession
to postpone	vertagen
ϟ to get one's act together	sein Leben in den Griff bekommen

Mulligan smiled again. "Mr Silver, we are not members of the drug squad. What Mr Marks does in the privacy of his own home is his business. But Mr Tyne was less tolerant of his... habit?"
A nod. "Rick would occasionally come in to recording sessions totally stoned, and we would have to postpone the recording. To begin with, Paul was quite patient, but just recently, Rick's 'habit', as you call it, had been getting a bit out of control. Paul lost his temper a couple of weeks ago and told Rick that if he didn't get his act together, he was going to hire a new drummer."
"And could he do that without everyone's agreement?"
"No, but to be quite honest, we've all got a bit tired of Rick's behaviour recently. It's not only a waste of our time, but it also involves huge costs. We have to pay for the recording studio, even though we don't use it."

The last note in Mulligan's notebook read: "RM drug addict, unpopular with PT et al, motive?"

Exercise 51: Questions about the text. **Beantworten Sie die Fragen zum Text in ganzen Sätzen!**

1. Why has Rick been causing problems for the band recently?

   ____

2. How did Sam feel about Paul?

   ____

3. Who knew about Esther's engagement to Paul?

   ____

4. Did Sam offer the detectives anything to drink?

   ____

5. How did Esther feel in the cellar?

   ____

"So what about Bill, Jean and Susan..." Mulligan opened his notebook to a new page.
Sam got up and walked over to the kitchen to pour himself another coffee.
"Bill and Jean had no problems with Paul," Sam remarked. "In fact, both of them worshipped the ground Paul walked on."

"So they would also have a reason to hate the person who killed Paul?"

Sam threw the spoon that he had just stirred his coffee with into the sink – a little too aggressively, Mulligan thought.

"For heaven's sake, Mr Mulligan! We all have a reason to hate Paul's murderer, but does that make us all murderers, too? Anyway, I thought it was certain that the murderer was Esther. Or do you think someone else was involved?"

"Everyone is innocent until proven guilty," Mulligan replied. "Anyway, it is not yet one hundred per cent certain that Esther Radcliffe committed the murder."

Even the seasoned inspector was surprised at the change of expression this comment produced in Sam Silver's face. It was as if somebody had told him that he had just won a million pounds.

"You're very fond of Esther Radcliffe, aren't you, Mr Silver?" Mulligan stated.

The pianist rubbed his hands together and did not immediately meet the inspector's eye.

et al	und andere
to worship	anbeten
seasoned	*hier*: erfahren, gestanden

"I'm afraid I regularly fall in love with Paul's girlfriends, Inspector. We have very similar tastes. When we were kids, I often used to date the girls Paul had jilted. They never normally noticed me until then."

Another note was scribbled in the notebook, "SS X ER; Motive?"

"And one last question, Mr Silver. How would you describe Susan Ellington?"

Sam Silver scowled. "To be honest with you, Inspector, I don't like her much! Susan is a good backing vocalist, but she's a bit of a prima donna without the talent. She really believes that she can take over where Esther left off, but her voice is nowhere near as good as Esther's. If you don't prove Esther's innocence soon, I will have to leave the band!"

In the car a few minutes later, Dawson turned to Mulligan. "So, what do you think?"
Mulligan grinned. "Well, even if we're not quite sure who did commit the murder, at least we have quite a few people with a motive."

Exercise 52: Future forms. Unterstreichen Sie die richtige Zukunftsform!

1. I am going / will go back to Plymouth at 6 p.m. today.
2. According to the weather forecast, it will / is going to continue raining tomorrow.
3. I am so scared, I think I will / am going to be sick.
4. If he asks her to marry him, she will / is going to say yes.
5. Oh dear, I've dropped my coffee. I am going to / will clear it up.

In her prison, Esther had stripped off most of her clothing. She was not sure what was worse. After having almost drowned during the night, the growing heat meant she was now almost suffocating in an airless vacuum of damp leaves and wet clothing. She had to get out. Suddenly she saw a nail on the floor and had an idea. She picked it up. It always worked in films, Esther thought, looking at the long rusty nail she had in her hand and then at the small keyhole in the wooden door. And what else did she have to do to pass the time?

Mulling on her thoughts and fears would only drive her crazy. And she was already worrying about another night in the cell. She pulled the mattress over to the door and, kneeling on it, put the nail into the lock and started moving it back and forth.

Richard Marks' flat was a dark mess. It smelt as though the windows had not been opened since Christmas, and there was the distinctive smell of marijuana in the air.

The drummer was unhealthily pale, and this was not helped by the fact that he was dressed all in black.

"Good morning, Mr Marks."

"What do you want?" he answered, without returning their greeting.

distinctive	charakteristisch
to bow	sich verbeugen
worn-out	abgenutzt
to dump	abladen

"We would like to ask you a couple of questions, Mr Marks," answered Mulligan. "We can do it here, or you can come down to the station later."

"Oh, what a great choice," he retorted sarcastically. "Can you wait here a second, I'll just go and get the silver out."

He closed the door on the detectives, and there was the sound of him throwing things into cupboards and opening windows. Then the door opened again.

"Please do come in," he bowed sarcastically.

The two officers followed the drummer into a small sitting room with three very worn-out sofas. On one of them, he had dumped a huge pile of old music magazines.

Rick sat or rather lay down on the second sofa, while Mulligan and Dawson perched on the edge of the third one.

"So, what do you want to know?"

"How well did you know Paul Tyne and Esther Radcliffe?" Mulligan started.

"Well enough," Rick replied.

Exercise 53: Odd one out. **Welches Wort ist das „schwarze Schaf"? Unterstreichen Sie!**

1. fiancée | best man | funeral | bride
2. embarrassed | confused | upset | sad
3. worship | like | adore | admire
4. beginner | veteran | experienced | seasoned
5. deserted | empty | run-down | vacant

"And how did you get on with them?" Detective Inspector Mulligan asked calmly.
"I like Esther a lot. She has a great voice, and she is a wonderful person to work with."
"And Paul Tyne?"
"He was okay."
"So you had no difficulties with him."
Richard Marks directed a penetrating gaze at the detective.
"I take it chatterbox Susan has told you that he and I were not getting on particularly well just before he died. That is true, but that doesn't mean I have anything to do with the murder."

Exercise 54: Verb forms. **Lesen Sie weiter und setzen Sie die richtige Verbform ein!**

Mulligan 1. notice ______________ that Richard Marks 2. be ______________ very nervous – and that the nervousness **3.** start _______________ after he **4.** mention _______________ Susan Ellington's name. "I **5.** also find out _______________ that you left London for a day after Paul Tyne's funeral. Where did you go?"

Richard Marks was now as white as a ghost.
"And did Susan tell you that, too?"
"It is not important who gave me the information, Mr Marks," replied Mulligan quietly. "However, I do need to know where you went."
"Why, didn't she tell you?" Rick asked sarcastically.
"I want you to tell me." Mulligan turned over a page in his notebook.
"You know as well as I do that I drove to Plymouth," Rick retorted angrily. "But I bet the bitch didn't tell you that the only reason I went to Plymouth was because of an e-mail she had received from Esther earlier on."
Dawson breathed in sharply, but more or less successfully managed to turn it into a yawn.

penetrating gaze	durchdringender Blick
chatterbox	Plaudertasche
yawn	Gähnen
of all people	ausgerechnet

"Ah yes, the e-mail…," Mulligan continued turning the pages in his notebook, avoiding any eye contact. "Perhaps you would like to tell me about it."
"Nothing much to tell. Esther sent Susan a mail asking her to explain what had happened. Apparently, Esther woke up in the hospital without being able to remember anything – and ran when she realized that she was the prime suspect in a murder case."
Richard Marks laughed nastily. "The fact that she contacted Susan of all people seems to confirm that Esther's memory is damaged."

"Which is why you went down to Plymouth to see Esther?"
"Susan gave my telephone number to Esther and told her to phone me. I actually drove all the way to Plymouth and stayed in a really cheap hotel. I was so sure that she would contact me, but she didn't. Susan hasn't heard from her either."

Achtung false friends

to wink	≠	winken
to wink		zwinkern
to wave		winken

"Cold feet, probably," commented Mulligan, snapping his notebook shut and winking (i) at Dawson. "I'm sorry, Mr Marks, but you will have to accompany us down to the station after all."

Exercise 55: Antonyms. **Welches Wort bedeutet das Gegenteil? Kreuzen Sie an!**

1. remember
a) ❒ recall
b) ❒ forget
c) ❒ recollect

2. terror
a) ❒ fear
b) ❒ horror
c) ❒ hope

3. beg
a) ❒ order
b) ❒ ask for
c) ❒ plead

4. anger
a) ❒ rage
b) ❒ calm
c) ❒ fury

5. trapped
a) ❒ caught
b) ❒ locked in
c) ❒ free

The first nail had broken, but there were plenty of rusty nails in the cell. Esther's fear that she would have to stay another night trapped in this horrible place kept her going. Her memory of Susan had also become clearer, and that, too, helped drown her fear – in rage. Over the next few hours, she pleaded with the door, screamed at it, kicked and scratched it, but the nail continued to be a nail and not a key. Just as she had started crying again, wiggling the nail around madly in frustration and rage, something clicked.

to plead	anflehen
to wiggle	wackeln

Esther fell out into another dark room.

8 COCK-AND-BULL STORIES

It was about 1:00 p.m. when the doorbell rang. Expecting it to be the postman, Susan opened the door with a friendly smile on her face. When she saw Detective Inspector Mulligan and Detective Sergeant Dawson on the doorstep, her smile froze.

"Detectives...," she stuttered. "What a surprise."

"Good afternoon, Ms Ellington," Mulligan said loudly, aware of the finely dressed neighbour walking past with her Yorkshire terrier. "I need to ask a few more questions about Esther Radcliffe. May I come in for a few minutes?"

"Yes, yes, of course," replied Susan. "Please come in." She shut the door hurriedly behind them, and the two detectives followed her into an amazing penthouse lounge with a fantastic view of the London skyscape. Sitting in the immaculately furnished room, which looked as if it had been taken straight out of House & Garden,[i] was Andrew Button. Like Susan Ellington, he was simply, but very expensively dressed.

House & Garden ist ein beliebtes Hochglanzmagazin zum Thema Wohnen.

Andrew Button quickly concealed his surprise and shock at seeing them with a broad, white smile.

"Detective Inspector Mulligan, Detective Sergeant Dawson, this is an unexpected pleasure. Would you like to sit down? May I get you something to drink? Some coffee or water? Or a beer? Susan, darling, could you please be so kind and…"

Mulligan shook his head. "Perhaps we could all sit down for a moment," he responded, turning round to Susan.

↯ cock-and-bull story	Lügengeschichte
furnished	möbliert
to conceal sth.	etw. verbergen
attempted murder	versuchter Mord
to utter	sich äußern
↯ to pass the buck	die Verantwortung abschieben
accusation	Vorwurf

Susan sat down next to Andrew, and Mulligan joined them, while Dawson remained standing.

"I hope that you have good news for us," Andrew asked. "Have you found Esther?"

"No, Mr Button, but we have reason to believe that Mr Marks is behind the murder of both Paul Tyne and the attempted murder of Esther Radcliffe."

"Rick!!" Susan Ellington's face blushed almost as dark a red as her lipstick. "What do you mean?"

"Richard Marks informed me that you received an e-mail from her."

Susan opened her mouth to answer the question, but before she could utter a word, Mulligan continued.

"Of course, we realized he was lying and just trying to pass the buck."

Andrew Button stared across at Susan sympathetically. "Poor Susan. Rick probably just pretended that Esther had contacted Susan and told her that she had lost her memory."

Mulligan also smiled sympathetically.

"Yes, exactly. Anyway, I do just have to check his accusation for the records. Where were you after Paul Tyne's funeral?"

Andrew's smile disappeared, and his face took on a sad expression.

Exercise 56: Verb phrases. Lesen Sie weiter und setzen Sie die korrekte Verbform ein. Achten Sie auf die Wortstellung!

"Susan and I **1.** be depressed very naturally ______________________________," he said. "So we came back here and stayed in the flat for the best part of the day. Our old neighbour, Mrs Huxley, **2.** can confirm probably ______________________________ that. We had the music on a bit too loud, and she **3.** tell afterwards us ______________________________ that she **4.** bang several times ______________________________ on the door, but we didn't hear. I must admit that we did smoke a bit of pot. That **5.** explain probably ______________________________ our deafness."

"Oh, yes, of course," Mulligan smiled, winking. "Don't worry. That is none of my business. As I said, I just needed your statement for the records."
"Of course, Inspector," said Andrew. "If we can be of any further assistance, please let us know."
"I don't think that will be necessary," Mulligan replied. "We have our murderer."
"Well, thank goodness," Susan replied.

"What was that all about?" Dawson glared at Mulligan in the car. "You don't believe Richard Marks committed the murder, do you?"
"No, I don't," replied Mulligan. "But I just wanted to check."
"And now you know?"
"Yes, or did you tell Andrew Button that the mail mentioned anything about a lost memory?"

Inside the flat, Andy's face was black with anger – and Susan knew better than to contradict him.
"That was a bloody stupid idea of yours, Susan." Andy slammed his glass down on the coffee table. "We should have just killed her straight away. And what was the idea with Sam? I told you Rick would have been a more logical choice."
"But I like Rick," answered Susan sulkily. "Anyway, I sent an anonymous letter about Sam to Inspector Mulligan."
"Oh, for heaven's sake," Andy exploded. "Do you ever use that bird brain of yours? Rick would have been the perfect scapegoat. He has a motive and even drove down to Plymouth. Now you have just confused things. What if they find Esther?"

sulkily	schmollend
scapegoat	Sündenbock
to flinch	zurückweichen
to crouch	sich ducken
to detect	orten, wahrnehmen

Susan paled. "Do you want to go back?"
Andy's blue eyes fixed Susan with the intensity of a hungry wolf. Susan flinched as if in pain when he stared at her and spat, "What do you think, you little idiot!"

After finally opening the door of her cell, Esther crouched in terror in the dark corridor for a couple of seconds, trying to detect any noises that warned of danger. As her eyes adapted to the new darkness, she was able to see the outline of a door at the top of some stairs. Her heart felt as though it was beating as loudly as a drum. As quietly as she could, she made her way up the stairs and to the door. Again, she listened.

Silence.

Please be open, she prayed, as she turned the handle. Yes!

Another corridor, this time in daylight. She was in a **derelict** house she realized. Broken glass, stones and **abandoned** pieces of furniture littered the floor. The front door was blowing back and forth on its **hinges**

Exercise 57: Since, for, ago? Ergänzen Sie die Zeitbegriffe!

1. Sam has known Paul's family ________ his school days.
2. Esther met Paul ten years ________
3. Rick has known Susan ________ ten years.
4. Jean has lived in London ________ 1989.
5. She has lived in London ________ over twenty years.

Perhaps it was just a trick to make her feel at ease, Esther thought. Picking up a piece of wood from the floor and **brandishing** it like a weapon, she continued down the corridor to the front door. The two metres felt more like two miles.

Both rooms on either side of the corridor were empty. Part of the wall was missing in the room on the right, and Esther could see the Cornish countryside around her. Feeling slightly less frightened, she walked through the front door and then slowly around the house. Everything suddenly seemed so normal outside her prison she almost smiled. But then she saw the empty tin of Red Bull lying on the ground next to an old bench, together with some **dog-ends**. These cigarettes had clearly been smoked by a woman wearing dark red lipstick – Susan's dark red lipstick. And Andy was more or less addicted to Red Bull. Yes, as she lay inside her cell, they had actually sat there and smoked a cigarette. She was **stunned** by their apparent cold-bloodedness.

derelict	verfallen
abandoned	zurückgelassen
hinge	Scharnier
to brandish	schwingen (Waffe)
↯ dog-end	Zigarettenkippe
stunned	fassungslos

Exercise 58: True or false? Welche Aussagen sind korrekt? Markieren Sie mit richtig ✓ oder falsch –!

1. Susan and Andrew admit that they were in Plymouth. ❐
2. The world seemed very strange to Esther when she came out of the house. ❐
3. Esther was in an old, ruined house. ❐
4. She had a proper weapon. ❐
5. The tin of Red Bull gives Andy away. ❐

With a shock, Esther realized that it was Andy's back that she had seen on the night of Paul's murder. He had killed Paul – and Susan had helped him. Tears of rage and incomprehension ran down her face. How could they do such a thing?
"Why?" she shouted. "Why?"

"So, what do we do now?" Dawson asked biting hungrily into a Cornish pasty[i] that he had bought on the way back to Scotland Yard. "How do we catch them now? And how were you so sure that it wasn't Richard Marks?"
"Instinct, I suppose," replied Mulligan. "And the fact that he and Susan Ellington were the only two with a real motive."
"So, why didn't you arrest them?"
"Because we don't have any firm evidence to connect either of them with the murder yet. I also believe they might know where Esther Radcliffe is, and I want them to lead me to her. That is why they are under 24-hour surveillance."

Cornish pasties sind eine britische Spezialität – Teigtaschen gefüllt mit Hackfleisch und Gemüse.

Exercise 59: Translation. Lesen Sie weiter und übersetzen Sie!

At Scotland Yard, Jean Jary and Bill Perez sat down in front of the inspector.

"Good morning, Ms Jary, Mr Perez," Mulligan 1. begrüßte ______________ them brightly. "You'll be glad to hear that we believe your story, due to the fact that we are of the

2. Meinung ______________ that Andrew Button and Susan Ellington are the **3. Hauptverdächtige** ______________ for the murder and **4. versuchter** ______________ murder."

"Andy and Susan?" Bill Perez **5. stotterte** ______________.

"Yes. We **6. glauben** ______________ that they know a lot more than they are telling us. We need you to help us..."

"Of course," Bill Perez and Jean Jary answered **7. gleichzeitig** ______________.

The house was out in the middle of nowhere. Esther had to cover quite a few miles before she found a road. When she did, she just started walking in the downhill direction, which she hoped would bring her back to the sea. As she wandered along, she thought back to the night of the murder. She remembered lying on the sofa, incapable of moving anywhere and feeling very ill. Had Susan and Andy come back and somehow got into an argument with Paul?

evidence	Beweis(e)

A car hooted. Esther saw that a middle-aged woman in a Range Rover had stopped on the side of the road.
"Are you alright? Have you had an accident?"
"Yes," Esther answered automatically.
"Jump in, then," shouted the woman. "I'll give you a lift. Don't worry about the dogs; their bark is worse than their bite."

She pointed at two barking Labradors in the back seat.
Esther gratefully got into the car, and the Barbour-coated lady sped down the hill. In less than half an hour, they were in Saltash, and the woman dropped Esther off almost on her doorstep.
Esther was in luck. Her key was still in her pocket. Andy and Sue had not taken it. Esther went inside. Totally exhausted, she lay down on the bed and closed her eyes.
In this room, she felt safe, but who could she trust now? She was going to have to contact someone, but who? Jean? Bill? Sam? Rick? She mumbled the names as she slipped into a deep sleep.

Exercise 60: Idioms. **Welche Definition passt zu den folgenden Redewendungen? Setzen Sie ein!**

to organize one's life | to be talented

a load of lies | terrified | to blame sb.

1. cock-and-bull story ______________
2. pass the buck ______________
3. white as a ghost ______________
4. get one's act together ______________
5. have what it takes ______________

Mulligan had told Jean Jary and Bill Perez to inform Andrew Button and Susan Ellington that Richard Marks had been charged and a confused woman – thought to be Esther Radcliffe – discovered.
Mulligan had worked for long enough in the business. If a kidnapper heard that his victim had been discovered, he or she would want to

check to make sure that the facts were right. It would be important when preparing for any additional questions.

Where Mulligan was wrong was in assuming that the two would take one of their own cars, which were parked in front of the flat. They had been focused on these vehicles, so it was only thanks to PC Rawlins that they did not miss the suspects' departure altogether.

In Großbritannien gehört das Kennzeichen zum Auto. Eine Ummeldung bei Verkauf oder Wohnortwechsel ist unnötig. Die ersten vier Buchstaben und Ziffern kennzeichnen Ort und Zeitraum der Erstzulassung.

"Sir, I've just seen them coming out of the underground car park in a black minivan, registration LK01 STM. (i) They'll be passing you any second now."

Mulligan and Dawson ducked as they saw the minivan turn the corner. After it had passed them, they pulled out and started to follow it. As they expected, it was driving towards Cornwall.

"Find out who owns the van and get back to me asap."

There was a lot of traffic on the road, so it was easy to trail the van with one or two other cars in between. Just as they were passing the intersection to Bath, Rawlins phoned back.

"So what did you find out?"

"It's a hire car, sir. Andrew Button picked it up on Tuesday, and a blonde woman was caught by a speed camera on the same day…"

to trail	verfolgen
intersection	Kreuzung
speed camera	Radarfalle
to keep sb. on tenterhooks	jdn. auf die Folter spannen
ϟ cheeky bugger	Frechdachs
to chuckle	schmunzeln, in sich hineinlachen

"Okay, Rawlins, don't keep me on tenterhooks, where was it?"

"Plymouth, sir."

"You know, Rawlins, I think we might get on, after all!"

"It would certainly make it easier for me to sleep, sir!"

Mulligan hung up. "Cheeky bugger!" he chuckled.

Exercise 61: Crossword puzzle. Lösen Sie das Kreuzworträtsel!

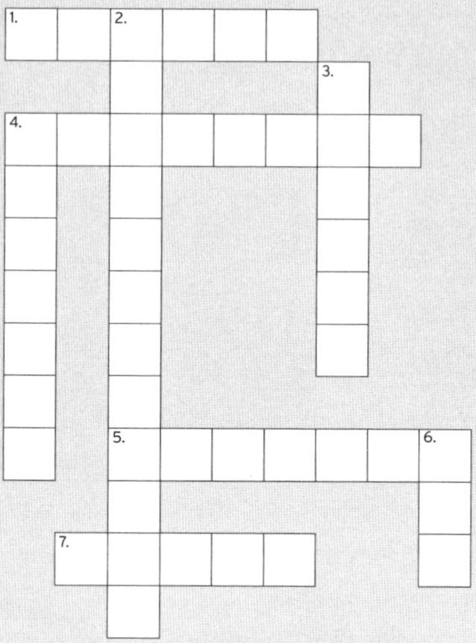

Across

1. A person who operates a vehicle
4. A wide road with several lanes where you can drive very fast
5. Word for vehicles and pedestrians on a road
7. A large vehicle for carrying goods

Down

2. A place where two roads cross each other
3. A policeman who makes sure that traffic rules are obeyed is a ... .
4. A vehicle, bigger than a car, with up to 7 seats
6. A vehicle with 4 wheels

Outside Plymouth, on the country roads, it started to get a bit more difficult for the detectives to trail the suspects at a discreet distance. Mulligan asked for some assistance from his colleagues in Plymouth, and soon there were three cars pursuing the minivan at different distances.

It was Detective Sergeant Bedford who eventually saw the minivan turn off the road and park behind a derelict house.

"They're outside at the moment, collecting rubbish by the looks of things," he told the others.

more like it	schon eher

"Evidence more like it," answered Mulligan, as he drew up behind the other car. "I think we can safely assume that Esther Radcliffe is locked in the house somewhere. As soon as they go inside, we are going to have to move fast. It could be a question of life or death. Dawson, Bedford and I will go inside. The others will stay outside to cut off their escape route. And secure their car."

Everyone nodded.

"They're going in now, sir," whispered Bedford.

"Right, lads. Let's go."

Six officers ran across the overgrown grass to the door. Mulligan, Dawson and Bedford quickly entered and moved as quietly as they could along the corridor. There was the sound of two people arguing loudly in the cellar.

"She can't have escaped! The door was locked. We both checked it."

"Well, Susan, unless she is hiding down the toilet, I really have no idea where she is," came the angry reply. "You should have let me kill her as I wanted. That bitch has caused us enough problems over the last few years."

"At least she may still believe that Sam killed Paul and kidnapped her, though – and that I was forced into helping him."

"Are you so sure? And what if her memory has come back?"

"This is all such a mess," Susan sighed.

"Yes, indeed," agreed Mulligan, as he walked in with his gun pointed straight at Andrew Button. "Put your hands where I can see them. You too, Ms Ellington."

When Susan saw the policeman behind her, she started whimpering like a puppy.

It took another twelve hours before Esther realized that she was no longer a fugitive. Seven of those twelve hours had been spent sound asleep in a warm, dry bed, but even rested it was difficult for her to believe that the nightmare was coming to an end. She stared at the announcement on the BBC website for a long time before she got dressed, walked to the nearest public phone and called the police station. She was put straight through to Inspector Mulligan.

"This is Esther Radcliffe..."

There was a moment of surprised silence, then a deep, rather dry voice answered her.

to whimper	wimmern
puppy	Welpe
fugitive	Flüchtige
superficially	auf den ersten Blick
to come to terms with sth.	etw. bewältigen

"Ah, yes, I was rather hoping you would call, Ms Radcliffe. You're a difficult lady to get hold of."

He sent a car for her. She made a statement, and the inspector insisted that she let the car take her all the way back to her home in London. It was as simple as that – superficially at least.

Of course, Esther found it far more difficult to come to terms with her grief and the betrayal by two people she had worked with for so long.

For months her mood fluctuated between sorrow and anger. The trial was a nightmare because she had to relive everything all over again.

For many months, she refused to sing, but with time Sam was able to persuade her to return to the stage.

Exercise 62: Translation. Welche Übersetzung stimmt? Kreuzen Sie an!

1. It was Rick who eventually did it.

a) ❒ Es war Rick, der es eventuell gemacht hat.

b) ❒ Es war Rick, der es vielleicht getan hat.

c) ❒ Es war Rick, der es schließlich gemacht hat.

2. You should have let me do it.

a) ❒ Sie müssen mich das machen lassen.

b) ❒ Sie hätten mich das machen lassen sollen.

c) ❒ Sie sollen mich das machen lassen.

3. She wouldn't have escaped if you had locked the door.

a) ❒ Sie wird nicht entkommen, wenn du die Tür abschließt.

b) ❒ Sie wäre nicht entkommen, wenn du die Tür abgeschlossen hättest.

c) ❒ Sie ist entkommen, weil du die Tür nicht abgeschlossen hast.

When asked after the trial whether she was happy with the verdict, Esther replied that nothing would bring her dead fiancé back. Secretly, however, it helped her to know that Andy and Susan were now experiencing her nightmare first-hand. Sometimes she imagined them at night putting their hands through the bars of their cells and crying out for mercy.

verdict	Urteil
mercy	Gnade

Exercise 63: Questions about the text. **Beantworten Sie die Fragen zum Text in ganzen Sätzen!**

1. Where were Paul Tyne's murderers arrested?

___

2. How did Esther discover that she was no longer a fugitive?

___

3. Why was it so difficult for Esther to recover from what happened?

___

4. Did Esther ever sing again?

___

5. What was the only thing that helped her after it was all over?

___

FINAL TEST

Exercise 1: Hidden words. Hier verstecken sich sechs Begriffe, die mit der Aufklärung eines Verbrechens zu tun haben!

D	N	G	Z	C	K	C	W	E	M	K
A	R	F	O	R	E	N	S	I	C	S
B	E	S	M	I	P	R	T	N	D	U
I	P	V	E	M	T	L	F	S	U	S
W	J	G	U	E	B	H	Q	P	V	P
C	O	N	S	T	A	B	L	E	G	E
G	O	S	E	Q	U	M	E	C	F	C
S	T	A	T	E	M	E	N	T	E	T
L	I	W	I	Q	P	L	X	O	H	Y
U	A	B	H	K	G	E	Q	R	L	B

Exercise 2: Verb forms. Vervollständigen Sie den Bericht in der Lokalzeitung Plymouth Herald!

Esther Radcliffe, the lead singer of Ballads and Balladies, 1. release ________________ from police custody yesterday. Originally 2. think ________________ to have murdered her agent Paul Tyne, it 3. since discover ________________ that the real murderers were two other members of the band: singer Susan Ellington and guitarist Andrew Button. Detective Inspector Mulligan, who 4. lead ________________ the investigations, told this newspaper that the main motive 5. appear to be ________________ envy.

Exercise 3: Match up the word pairs. Was gehört zusammen? Ordnen Sie zu!

1. ☐ surgeon	a) recording studio
2. ☐ nurse	b) front desk
3. ☐ detective	c) hideaway
4. ☐ musician	d) operating room
5. ☐ receptionist	e) crime scene
6. ☐ kidnapper	f) ward

Exercise 4: Idioms. **Ergänzen Sie die Redewendungen und enträtseln Sie das Lösungswort!**

1. mad — _ _ _ [ ] _ as a fruitcake
2. fast asleep — _ [ ] _ _ to the world
3. sleep on the streets — sleep [ ] _ _ _ _
4. lose patience — at the end of one's _ _ _ _ _ [ ]
5. not honestly sad — cry _ _ [ ] _ _ _ _ _ _ tears
6. go on determined despite difficulties — _ [ ] _ _ one's teeth

Lösung: _ _ _ _ _ _

Exercise 5: Choose the correct quantifier. **Wählen Sie jeweils die richtige Mengenbezeichnung!**

1. Esther did not have many / much alternatives when she wanted to escape.
2. She did not have many / much money either.
3. Susan spent a lot of / much money in the town.
4. There were only a few / little people in the train going to Plymouth.
5. Sam loves German composers, but can speak little / few German.

Exercise 6: False friends. Wählen Sie die richtige Übersetzung!

1. Susan Ellington ist kein sensibler Mensch.

a) ❒ Susan Ellington is not a very sensible person.

b) ❒ Susan Ellington is not a very sensitive person.

2. Aktuell ist sie auf der Flucht.

a) ❒ She is currently on the run.

b) ❒ She is actually on the run.

3. PC Rawlins wird das eventuell schaffen.

a) ❒ PC Rawlins will succeed eventually.

b) ❒ PC Rawlins will possibly succeed.

4. Esther winkt ihren Fans zu.

a) ❒ Esther winks at her fans.

b) ❒ Esther waves at her fans.

5. Andrew hat sich blamiert.

a) ❒ Andrew made a fool of himself.

b) ❒ Andrew blamed himself.

ANSWERS

Exercise 1: **1.** isn't she **2.** did she **3.** haven't you **4.** would she **5.** aren't I

Exercise 2: **1.** in **2.** against **3.** take **4.** matter

Exercise 3: **1.** move **2.** hurry **3.** remember **4.** window **5.** dead **6.** nurse
Lösung: murder

Exercise 4: **1.** broken **2.** fast **3.** lose **4.** happily **5.** off **6.** at

Exercise 5: **1.** d **2.** c **3.** a **4.** e **5.** b

Exercise 6: **1.** (wieder)erkennen **2.** kichern **3.** verstecken **4.** beruhigen **5.** die Stirn runzeln

Exercise 7:
2. She asked her what she was going to do.
3. He said that they would take her home soon.
4. She said that people in disguise always wore a hat.
5. She said that she was very young.

Exercise 8: **1.** turned **2.** could **3.** discover **4.** began **5.** walked **6.** parked

Exercise 9: **1.** frightened **2.** rudely **3.** carefully **4.** taxi **5.** think

Exercise 10: **1.** passenger **2.** copy **3.** space **4.** travellers **5.** while

Exercise 11: **1.** much **2.** many **3.** many **4.** much **5.** much, many

Exercise 12: **Across:** swimsuit, passport
Down: suitcase, tickets, money, guide

Exercise 13: **1.** ledge **2.** receptionist **3.** innocence **4.** pensioner **5.** suspicious

Exercise 14: **1.** luxuriously **2.**well **3.** loud **4.** guilty **5.** easily

Exercise 15: **1.** anxiously **2.** how **3.** anywhere **4.** too **5.** nobody **6.** at least

Exercise 16: **1.** false (She was seen at Paddington Station.) **2.** true **3.** false (No, she wanted to find a safer hiding place.) **4.** true **5.** true

Exercise 17: **1.** interviewed **2.** escaped **3.** have never been **4.** didn't sell **5.** have known

Exercise 18: **1.** I don't want to be by myself.
2.You've got to help me.
3. I haven't got anybody.
4. I don't know.
5. Got you! (auch: "Ich verstehe.")

Exercise 19: **1.** unhealthy **2.** intolerant **3.** irregular **4.** impolite **5.** dishonest **6.** non-smoker

Exercise 20: **1.** past **2.** until **3.** to **4.** on **5.** of

Exercise 21: **1.** had given **2.** saw **3.** had never seen **4.** went

Exercise 22: **1.** woman **2.** in **3.** stay **4.** cost **5.** breakfast

Exercise 23:

1. S	2. A	3. L	4. T	5. A	6. S	7. H
22. O	23. L	24. I	25. T	26. E	27. V	8. O
21. P	36. R	37. S	38. E	39. S	28. E	9. R
20. O	35. U	42. D	41. N	40. A	29. N	10. R
19. T	34. N	33. U	32. G	31. N	30. I	11. O
18. C	17. E	16. P	15 S	14. U	13. S	12. R

Exercise 24: **1.** hair **2.** pathologist **3.** committed **4.** weighs **5.** drugs **6.** file

Exercise 25: **2.** If I had a good voice, I would sing.
3. If we had a lead singer, we would perform at Marco's.
4. If I knew his parents, I would speak at his funeral.
5. If they weren't all in shock, they would know what to do.

Exercise 26: **1.** had fallen **2.** getting 3 didn't know **4.** as bad as **5.** comparison

Exercise 27: **1.** nightmares **2.** resting **3.** gradually **4.** dislike **5.** confused

Exercise 28: **1.** surprised **2.** together **3.** obviously **4.** suppose **5.** probably

Exercise 29: **Across: 2.** Dawson **5.** suspect **6.** meet **8.** Rick **10.** TR **11.** Ladies
Down: 1. lipstick **3.** secret **4.** guitar **6.** murder **7.** train **9.** cell

Exercise 30: **2.** Dawson was making a phone call when PC Rawlins dropped a glass.
3. Paul was speaking to Esther when the murderer hit him with a lamp.
4. Mulligan was driving to work when his car broke down.
5. Mulligan was thinking about the case, when Jean Jary interrupted him.

Exercise 31: **1.** b **2.** c **3.** a.

Exercise 32: **1.** false (The church was quite full.) **2.** false (No, Paul's family doesn't blame them.) **3.** false (No, Sam spoke at the funeral.) **4.** true **5.** true **6.** false (Sam was Paul Tyne's best friend.) **7.** true **8.** false (No, they went to the studio.)

Exercise 33: **1.** e **2.** d **3.** a **4.** c **5.** b

Exercise 34: **1.** reminded **2.** remind **3.** remember **4.** remind **5.** remembered

Exercise 35: **1.** phoned **2.** Have you spoken **3.** Did you get **4.** haven't received **5.** was

Exercise 36: **1.** What was Inspector Mulligan thinking about?
2. When did the murder take place?
3. Where are Esther and Susan going to meet?
4. Who did Esther call?
5. Why will nobody notice them?

Exercise 37: **1.** clothing **2.** disappoint **3.** flowery **4.** frown **5.** cheerful **6.** report
Lösung: golfer

Exercise 38: **1.** mobile phone (handy) **2.** know (no) **3.** I asked you (have asked) **4.** disappeared **5.** registration numbers (registrar numbers)

Exercise 39: **1.** e **2.** c **3.** a **4.** b **5.** d

Exercise 40: Detective Inspector Mulligan was also still awake.
However, unlike Esther, he was sitting on a comfortable hotel bed and watching a late-night film.
He and Peter Dawson had eaten a nice meal in the hotel's restaurant.
They then arranged when to meet the following morning before going to their respective rooms.
Next to him, Mulligan had a notebook and a glass of whisky from the minibar.

Exercise 41: **1.** dry **2.** ignore **3.** increase **4.** story

Exercise 42: **1.** You **2.** her **3.** I **4.** you **5.** your **6.** him **7.** it

Exercise 43: **1.** in **2.** over **3.** up **4.** out **5.** about

Exercise 44: **Across: 1.** escape **5.** idea **7.** rag **9.** prisoner **10.** drown
Down: 2. season **3.** pew **4.** kidnapper **6.** search **8.** moon

Exercise 45: **1.** c **2.** e **3.** d **4.** a **5.** b

Exercise 46: **1.** When **2.** While **3.** As soon as **4.** whether **5.** as **6.** until **7.** if **8.** because

Exercise 47: **1.** The police blocked the road.
2. The kidnappers pulled Esther into the minivan.
3. The police told the witnesses to stay in town.
4. They arrested the murderer yesterday.
5. The jury found the accused guilty.
6. The murderer hit the victim with a lamp.

Exercise 48: **1.** an **2.** Every **3.** most of **4.** more quickly **5.** had to be

Exercise 49: **1.** false (No, she doesn't want to cause Esther any trouble.) **2.** false (The water doesn't rise above the sink.) **3.** true **4.** false (Mulligan wants to visit the band members at their homes.) **5.** true

Exercise 50: **1.** patiently **2.** investigating **3.** piece **4.** popular **5.** realized

Exercise 51: **1.** Rick's drug "habit" has been getting out of control recently.
2. Sam saw Paul as his best friend and he respected him as an agent.
3. The band members and Paul's parents knew about the engagement.
4. Sam offered the detectives some coffee.
5. Esther felt desperate and alone in the cellar - like a frightened animal.

Exercise 52: **1.** am going **2.** is going to **3.** am going to **4.** will **5.** will

Exercise 53: **1.** funeral **2.** sad **3.** like **4.** beginner **5.** run-down

Exercise 54: **1.** noticed **2.** was **3.** had started/started **4.** had mentioned **5.** also found out

Exercise 55: **1.** b **2.** c **3.** a **4.** b **5.** c

Exercise 56: **1.** were naturally very depressed **2.** can probably confirm **3.** told us afterwards **4.** had banged several times **5.** probably explains

Exercise 57: **1.** since **2.** ago **3.** for **4.** since **5.** for

Exercise 58: **1.** false (DI Mulligan doesn't ask them about Plymouth.) **2.** false (No, Esther is startled by how normal everything feels.) **3.** true **4.** false (No, Esther has grabbed a piece of wood.) **5.** true

Exercise 59: **1.** greeted **2.** opinion **3.** prime suspects **4.** attempted **5.** stuttered **6.** believe **7.** at the same time

Exercise 60: **1.** a load of lies **2.** to blame sb. **3.** terrified **4.** to organize one's life **5.** to be talented

Exercise 61: **Across: 1.** driver **4.** motorway **5.** traffic **7.** lorry
Down: 2. intersection **3.** warden **4.** minivan **6.** car

Exercise 62: **1.** c **2.** b **3.** b

Exercise 63: **1.** They were arrested in a cell.
2. She read an announcement on the BBC website.
3. It was difficult because of her grief over Paul's death and the betrayal by old friends.
4. Yes, she started singing again months later.
5. It helped her to know that Andy and Susan were living her nightmare.

FINAL TEST

Exercise 1: **Across:** forensics, constable, statement
Down: crime, inspector, suspect

Exercise 2: **1.** was released **2.** thought **3.** has since been discovered **4.** led **5.** appears to have been

Exercise 3: **1.** d **2.** f **3.** e **4.** a **5.** b **6.** c

Exercise 4: **1.** nutty **2.** dead **3.** rough **4.** tether **5.** crocodile **6.** grit
Lösung: terror

Exercise 5: **1.** many **2.** much **3.** a lot of **4.** a few **5.** little

Exercise 6: **1.** b **2.** a **3.** b **4.** b **5.** a

GLOSSARY

ϟ = umgangssprachlich
pl = Plural

abandoned	zurückgelassen
ϟ a bit of a handful	*hier*: etw. schwierig
accommodation	Unterkunft
account	*hier*: Bericht
accusation	Vorwurf
addiction	Sucht, Abhängigkeit
ϟ to add up	*hier*: Sinn ergeben, stimmen
aimlessly	ziellos
Alsatian	Deutscher Schäferhund
amber	bernsteinfarben
ample	reichlich, genügend
And pigs might fly!	Wer's glaubt, wird selig.
appearance	Aussehen
appropriate	angemessen, passend
asap (= as soon as possible)	schnellstmöglich
to assess	abschätzen, einschätzen
to assume	annehmen
at all events	auf alle Fälle
at a snail's pace	im Schneckentempo
attempted murder	versuchter Mord
auburn	rotbraun
backing vocalist	Backgroundsängerin
bar	*hier*: Gitterstab
barn	Scheune
to beam	strahlen

to be capable of	fähig sein
ϟ to be into sth.	auf etw. stehen/abfahren
beret	Baskenmütze
best man	Trauzeuge
betrayal	Verrat
to blush	erröten
boredom	Langeweile
to bow	sich verbeugen
to brandish	schwingen (Waffe)
to breathe a sigh of relief	erleichtert aufatmen
briskly	rasch, flott
to call in sick	sich krank melden
canvas	Leinwand
to carve	schnitzen
case	*hier*: Fall
to charge	*hier*: anklagen
chatterbox	Plaudertasche
ϟ cheeky bugger	Frechdachs
to chuckle	schmunzeln, in sich hineinlachen
clammy	feuchtkalt
clothes locker	Spind
coach	Reisebus
ϟ cock-and-bull story	Lügengeschichte
to come (came, come) round	zu sich kommen
to come to terms with sth.	etw. bewältigen
to commit sth.	etw. begehen
common	*hier*: Gemeindeland
compartment	Abteil
complimentary	*hier*: Gratis-, kostenlos
to compose oneself	sich beruhigen, sich fassen
to conceal sth.	etw. verbergen
concerned	besorgt
to confirm	bestätigen
constitution	Verfassung
convinced	überzeugt

courtyard	(Innen-)Hof
to cover sth.	über etw. berichten
crate	Kiste
to crawl	kriechen
to creak	knarren
to crouch	sich ducken
crumpled	zerknüllt
custody	Gewahrsam
cutlery	Besteck
damp	feucht
to dare	wagen
⚡ dead to the world	total hinüber
delighted	begeistert, erfreut
derelict	verfallen
to deserve	verdienen (Leistung)
to despise	verachten
detached	losgelöst, unbeteiligt
to detect	orten, wahrnehmen
determined	entschlossen
disinfectant	Desinfektionsmittel
distinctive	charakteristisch
to distract	ablenken
distractedly	zerstreut, unkonzentriert
dizzy	schwindelig
⚡ dog-end	Zigarettenkippe
donation	Spende
⚡ to do time	im Gefängnis sitzen
down-to-earth	bodenständig
draining board	Abtropfbrett
dread	Furcht, Grauen
to drown one's sorrows	seine Sorgen in Alkohol ertränken
⚡ drugged up to the eyeballs	total zugedröhnt
to dump	abladen
to dunk	eintunken

to dwindle	schwinden
to dye	färben
embarrassed	verlegen
to emerge	herauskommen, hervortreten
engaged	*hier*: verlobt
estuary	(Fluss-)Mündung, Meeresarm
et al	und andere
ether-soaked	in Äther getränkt
eve	Vorabend
evidence	Spuren, Beweise
exhausted	erschöpft
expletives	Schimpfwörter
exposed	exponiert, schutzlos
fiancé/-ée	Verlobter/-e
to find shelter	Schutz finden
firm	fest, bestimmt
to flash	blitzen
flight	*hier*: Stockwerk
to flinch	zurückweichen
flirtatious	kokett
to flood	durchfluten, überfluten
flustered	gestresst, nervös
the force	*hier*: (Polizei-)Truppe
forensics	Spurensicherung; Rechtsmedizin
to frame sb.	jdm. etw. anhängen
to freeze (froze, frozen)	*hier*: erstarren
to frogmarch	(im Polizeigriff) abführen
to frown	die Stirn runzeln
frumpy	altbacken
fugitive	Flüchtige(r)
to fume	vor Wut toben
furious	wütend
furnished	möbliert
ϟ to get one's act together	sein Leben in den Griff bekommen
to get on with sb.	sich mit jdm. gut verstehen

to giggle	kichern
ginger-haired	rothaarig
to give in	aufgeben
to give oneself up	sich (der Polizei) stellen
to glance	flüchtig blicken
to glare at sb.	jdn. anstarren
to grasp sth.	etw. (fest) fassen
gossip	Tratsch
gracious	*hier*: liebenswürdig
grand piano	Flügel
grief	Trauer
to grit one's teeth	die Zähne zusammenbeißen
to groan	stöhnen
to growl	knurren
to grumble	brummen, murren
grumpily	mürrisch
gullible	leichtgläubig
ϟ habit	Sucht
to handcuff	Handschellen anlegen
to have a go	etw. ausprobieren
ϟ to have what it takes	das Zeug zu etw. haben
to head (towards)	eine Richtung ansteuern
hedge	Hecke
Her heart sank.	Ihr rutschte das Herz in die Hose.
hinge	Scharnier
to hiss	zischen
to hitch up	hochziehen
hollow	Mulde, Vertiefung
to hoot	rufen (Eule)
hotplate	Kochplatte
to hum	summen
immaculately	makellos
impenetrable	unüberwindlich
to impersonate sb.	sich als jd. ausgeben
inconceivable	undenkbar

inconvenient	ungünstig, ungelegen
in conversational mood	gesprächig
in her mind's eye	vor ihrem geistigen Auge
innocence	Unschuld
intersection	Kreuzung
intriguing	faszinierend
investigation	Ermittlung
item	Gegenstand
It just goes to show...	Da sieht man mal wieder ...
jerk	Ruck, Zuckung
jet black	kohlrabenschwarz
jigsaw piece	Puzzlestück
to jilt	abservieren, den Laufpass geben
to jog sb.'s memory	jds. Gedächtnis nachhelfen
to jolt upright	hochschnellen
judging by	nach etw. zu urteilen
to jump	*hier*: zusammenzucken
ϟ to jump out of one's skin	sich zu Tode erschrecken
keen	eifrig
to keep sb. on tenterhooks	jdn. auf die Folter spannen
keys *pl*	Tasten
kitchenette	Kochnische
to knock over	umstoßen
ϟ lad	Bursche
landlady	Zimmerwirtin, Vermieterin
to launch into sth.	zu etw. ansetzen, sich auf etw. stürzen
ledge	Sims
let alone	ganz zu schweigen
ϟ to lie (lay, lain) low	untertauchen
limbs *pl*	Gliedmaßen
literally	buchstäblich, wortwörtlich
to lock sb. up	jdn. einsperren, jdn. wegsperren
loft residence	Loft
to long to	sich sehnen

to lose one's temper	wütend werden, in Zorn geraten
ϟ to make a racket	Krawall machen
to make a statement	eine Aussage machen
maze	Labyrinth
meek as a lamb	lammfromm
mercy	Gnade
to merge into	in der Menge aufgehen
to mill around	umherlaufen
moodily	launisch
more like it	schon eher
to mull over	sich durch den Kopf gehen lassen
murmur	Murmeln
musty	muffig
to mutter	murren, brummeln
nasty	*hier*: unangenehm; garstig, fies
neat	*hier*: pur
ϟ Never mind!	Egal! Was soll's!
newsstand	Zeitungskiosk
nightcap	Schlummertrunk, Absacker
nonetheless	nichtsdestotrotz
ϟ nutty as a fruitcake	total verrückt
to obstruct	behindern
of all people	ausgerechnet
to owe sb. sth.	jdm. etw. schuldig sein
pandemonium	Tumult
paralyzed	gelähmt
to pass out	bewusstlos werden
ϟ to pass the buck	die Verantwortung abschieben
ϟ peck	Küsschen
to peer	spähen
penetrating gaze	durchdringender Blick
to perch	hocken (wie ein Vogel)
persistence	Hartnäckigkeit
petrified	versteinert, starr vor Angst
pew	Kirchenbank

picturesque	malerisch
pitch black	pechschwarz
to play one's cards right	seine Trümpfe richtig ausspielen
to plead	anflehen
plump	pummelig
to postpone	vertagen
⚡ pot	Marihuana
to pour in	*hier*: nach und nach eintreffen
praise	Lob
predictable	berechenbar
to press one's luck	sein Schicksal herausfordern
to presume	davon ausgehen
prime suspect	Hauptverdächtige/r
proverbial	sprichwörtlich
to pry	herumschnüffeln
puppy	Welpe
⚡ to put one's foot in it	ins Fettnäpfchen treten
queue	Warteschlange
rag	Lumpen
to reach the end of one's tether	mit der Geduld am Ende sein
record	*hier*: Akte
recording session	Aufnahmesession
to recur	sich wiederholen
rehearsal	Probe
relieved	erleichtert
to relish	genießen, Gefallen finden an
respective	jeweilig, entsprechend
to retort	scharf erwidern
to rinse	auswaschen
ripple	kleine Welle, Plätschern
rodent	Nagetier
run-down	heruntergekommen
sachet	Beutel
scapegoat	Sündenbock

to scowl	finster blicken
to scribble	kritzeln
to scurry	huschen
seasoned	*hier*: gestanden, erfahren
to seep	sickern
sense	*hier*: Vernunft
sentence	*hier*: Strafe, Strafmaß
service	*hier*: Gottesdienst
⚡ shady	zwielichtig
shopping trolley	Einkaufswagen
to shudder	schaudern
siblings *pl*	Geschwister
to sink (sank, sunk) in	ins Bewusstsein dringen
to slam	zuknallen
to slap	eine Ohrfeige geben
to sleep it off	einen Rausch ausschlafen
to sleep rough	im Freien übernachten
to slump	zusammensacken
to slur	lallen
to snap	blaffen
to sneeze	niesen
to sniff	*hier*: schniefen
soaked to the skin	klatschnass
to sob	schluchzen
solitary	abgelegen, einsam
soothing	beruhigend
spacious	geräumig
speed camera	Radarfalle
to spill (spilt, spilt)	verschütten
split second	Bruchteil einer Sekunde
squashed	gequetscht
start	*hier*: Aufschrecken
startling	*hier*: außergewöhnlich
to starve	verhungern
stench	Gestank

to step up	verstärken
to stop dead in one's tracks	wie angewurzelt stehenbleiben
strand	*hier*: Strähne
stubbornly	hartnäckig, stur
stunned	fassungslos
suffocating	stickig
sulkily	schmollend
superficially	auf den ersten Blick
supporting beam	Stützbalken
to surge forward	nach vorne drängen
suspect	Verdächtigte(r)
suspicious	*hier*: misstrauisch
to swap	austauschen
to swear (swore, sworn)	*hier*: fluchen
ϟ to take a shine to sb.	einen Narren an jdm. fressen
to take its toll	Tribut fordern
to taunt	verhöhnen, sticheln
tearful	weinerlich
teeny weeny	klitzeklein
tenant	Mieter(in)
thud	dumpfer Aufschlag
thug	Schläger
thunderbolt	Blitzschlag
to tick off	abhaken
to tighten	*hier*: fester halten, verstärken
toddler	Kleinkind
traffic warden	Politesse, Verkehrspolizist
to trail	verfolgen
ϟ Trouble is brewing.	Es herrscht dicke Luft.
to tuck into	(mit Appetit) essen
to tune	(Instrument) stimmen
to turn out to be	sich entpuppen als
twitch	Zucken
unbearable	unerträglich
unconscious	bewusstlos

under police surveillance	polizeilich überwacht
up-and-coming star	Nachwuchsstar
to utter	sich äußern
verdict	Urteil
vote of confidence	Vertrauensbeweis
voucher	Gutschein
vulnerable	verwundbar
wary	vorsichtig, misstrauisch
to weave	*hier*: sich durchschlängeln
weeds *pl*	Unkraut
whereabouts	Verbleib, Aufenthaltsort
to whimper	wimmern
to whiz past	vorbeisausen
widow	Witwe
to wiggle	wackeln
with chattering teeth	zähneklappernd
word spread	es hat sich herumgesprochen
worn-out	abgenutzt
to worship	anbeten
wryly	ironisch, schief
yawn	Gähnen

LIST OF EXERCISES

Compact Lernkrimis auch in Spanisch, Französisch, Italienisch und Deutsch erhältlich.

Compact Lernkrimi Classic

A1

A2

B1

Das Rätsel der Mumie
ISBN 978-3-8174-7304-5

Deadly Mistake
ISBN 978-3-8174-8259-7

Der Rächer von Canterbury
ISBN 978-3-8174-7662-6

Der rote Nebel
ISBN 978-3-8174-7574-2

Die Jagd nach dem Vampir
ISBN 978-3-8174-7305-2

Ein fast perfekter Coup
ISBN 978-3-8174-7568-1

Game Over in Soho
ISBN 978-3-8174-7878-1

Im Schatten des Towers
ISBN 978-3-8174-7687-9

Komplott unter Palmen
ISBN 978-3-8174-7571-1

Schüsse im Nebel
ISBN 978-3-8174-7763-0

Tod eines Dandys
ISBN 978-3-8174-7660-2

Toxic Testament
ISBN 978-3-8174-7879-8

American English

Tod im Grand Canyon
ISBN 978-3-8174-7572-8

Sammelband 3 in 1 (B1/B2)

Inspector Hudson ermittelt
ISBN 978-3-8174-7625-1

London Crime Time
ISBN 978-3-8174-7787-6

B2

Das geheimnisvolle Gemälde
ISBN 978-3-8174-7306-9

Der Seelenjäger
ISBN 978-3-8174-7581-0

Der unheimliche Ritter
ISBN 978-3-8174-7661-9

Die genetische Falle
ISBN 978-3-8174-7569-8

Die Rache des Lords
ISBN 978-3-8174-7663-3

Die Spur des Höllenhundes
ISBN 978-3-8174-7307-6

Diebstahl im Morgengrauen
ISBN 978-3-8174-7638-1

Lady Mayfairs Rache
ISBN 978-3-8174-7815-6

Schatten der Vergangenheit
ISBN 978-3-8174-7570-4

Business English

Das letzte Roulette
ISBN 978-3-8174-7609-1

Der 25-Millionen-Coup
ISBN 978-3-8174-7659-6

Schmierige Geschäfte
ISBN 978-3-8174-7658-9

Teuflische Intrigen
ISBN 978-3-8174-7608-4

American English

Das Skyline-Syndikat
ISBN 978-3-8174-7573-5

C1/C2

A Scottish Murder Mystery
ISBN 978-3-8174-8379-2

Compact Lernkrimi
Kurzkrimis

Compact Lernkrimi
Lernthriller

Compact Lernkrimi Kurzkrimis	Compact Lernkrimi Lernthriller	
		A1
Blood and Breakfast ISBN 978-3-8174-7760-9 **Deadly Business** ISBN 978-3-8174-9215-2 **Endstation Waterloo Bridge** ISBN 978-3-8174-7733-3 **Es war Mord, my Lord** ISBN 978-3-8174-7734-0 **Mord at Teatime** ISBN 978-3-8174-7839-2		A2
Bullets over Bristol ISBN 978-3-8174-8544-4 **Death Comes Knocking** ISBN 978-3-8174-7945-0	**Faceless Killer** ISBN 978-3-8174-8856-8	B1
	In Terror ISBN 978-3-8174-8857-5	B2
		C1/C2

Compact Lernkrimi Rätselblock

Compact Lernkrimi Hörbuch

	Compact Lernkrimi Rätselblock	Compact Lernkrimi Hörbuch
A1		
A2	**The Art of Crime** ISBN 978-3-8174-9155-1	**A Shot in the Night** ISBN 978-3-8174-8202-3 **Death Wish** ISBN 978-3-8174-8204-7 **The Butterworth Mystery** ISBN 978-3-8174-8203-0
B1	**A Deadly Puzzle** ISBN 978-3-8174-8832-2	**Bloody Revenge** ISBN 978-3-8174-8860-5 **Das Mädchen von King's Cross** ISBN 978-3-8174-7673-2 **Der Themse-Mörder** ISBN 978-3-8174-7674-9
B2		**Blutige Erbschaft** ISBN 978-3-8174-7676-3 **Die Intrigantin** ISBN 978-3-8174-7675-6 **<u>Business English</u>** **Mord im Office** ISBN 978-3-8174-7747-0
C1/C2		

Compact Lernkrimi
Audio-Learning

Compact Lernkrimi
Sprachkurs

	Englisch für Anfänger (A1/A2) ISBN 978-3-8174-7784-5	A1
Verschollen im Dartmoor ISBN 978-3-8174-7796-8		A2
Totenstille im Hyde Park ISBN 978-3-8174-7797-5		B1
		B2
		C1/C2